MOODY

BIBLE

INSTITUTE

A Pictorial History

MOODY

BIBLE

INSTITUTE

A Pictorial History

BY BERNARD R. DE REMER

MOODY PRESS · CHICAGO

Facing title page

TOP: Chicago in 1883. From a lithograph by S. D. Childs and Co. Arrow indicates Chicago Avenue Church, in which many of the first Moody Bible Institute classes met.

Courtesy Chicago Historical Society

BOTTOM: Chicago lake front today. At extreme left is Prudential Building, newest skyscraper here. Arrow indicates M. B. I. buildings, strategically located one mile north of the famous Loop.

Aerial photo by Laurence R. Lowry. Reprinted by special permission from Holiday, *copyright 1956, by The Curtis Publishing Company.*

Front end papers

Group of Institute faculty members, visitors, and students, about 1892. In front row center is Dr. R. A. Torrey, first superintendent of M. B. I. On his left are Mrs. Torrey, A. F. Gaylord, and Dr. D. B. Towner. On Dr. Torrey's right is Mrs. Sarah B. Capron, first superintendent of women at M. B. I.

Rear end papers

M. B. I. faculty members (right foreground) and day school students, together with officials and employees, meet weekly for chapel in Torrey-Gray Auditorium.

Front row, left to right:

A. F. Broman, dean of men; Dr. Alfred Martin, dean of faculty; Dr. S. Maxwell Coder, vice president and dean of education; Henry C. Crowell, executive vice-president and general manager; Dr. William Culbertson, president; Ernest C. Christiansen, vice-president of Investments; Harold E. Stockburger, vice-president of Treasury Branch; Miss Gladys Mary Talbot, registrar; Miss Angelyn G. Dantuma, dean of women. Not shown are Robert L. Constable, vice-president of Development Branch, and LeRoy Johnson, treasurer.

Photo by John Ingram, October, 1959

Dedication

WILBUR M. SMITH

To my beloved former instructor

DR. WILBUR M. SMITH

this volume is gratefully dedicated. Without his consecrated zeal and devotion to "the school that D. L. Moody founded," there would probably never have been a Moodyana exhibit. Certainly he was the chief protagonist in its formative period.

Dr. Smith, son of Thomas S. Smith, attended Moody Bible Institute 1913-14, later Wooster (Ohio) College. After pastorates in Maryland, Virginia, and Pennsylvania, he joined the M.B.I. faculty in 1938. Thousands of former students recall with deepest appreciation the Doctrine and other classes when he revealed the hidden treasures of the Word of God in his own inimitable style.

In preparation for the 60th anniversary of the Institute in 1946, Dr. Smith was largely responsible for setting up an outstanding exhibit on the second floor of Crowell Hall de-

picting the life and work of D. L. Moody. This was the beginning of Moodyana in its present form. It now occupies the rooms used by D. L. Moody in the 153 building, with an exhibit of letters, photographs, sermon notes and other items pertaining to his life and work, and also to the founding and growth of M.B.I. One room has on display five historic organs owned by Ira D. Sankey and others.

Dr. Smith is the widely known author of 15 books, including the monumental *Annotated Bibliography of D. L. Moody*. He contributes articles to the *Sunday School Times* and to other periodicals and regularly provides a feature department for *Moody Monthly*. Since 1947, he has been professor of English Bible at Fuller Theological Seminary, Pasadena, Calif. He is a frequent speaker at Founder's Week, English Keswick and other conventions.

Contents

Introduction

It is fitting that this pictorial history should appear as Moody Bible Institute approaches its 75th anniversary. Though there have been articles and booklets about the Institute, this is the first attempt to tell M.B.I.'s wonderful history both by words and by authentic pictures. Mr. Bernard DeRemer, custodian of Moodyana and diligent student of all the history of the Institute, is to be commended for the excellent material he presents to us in this book.

It is an occasion of renewed thanksgiving to recall God's faithfulness in bringing into existence this school in the face of great difficulties, and in not only preserving it, but giving it an ever-expanding ministry down through the years.

This profusely illustrated volume will be treasured by all friends of the Institute, and especially by our former students. May our alumni be helped to walk in memory in the classrooms, to the assignments and through the hallowed days and happy occasions of their time of study here. May our many other friends be blessed as they see the evidence that God has blessed the school that D. L. Moody founded. May we continue to go on with God.

—WILLIAM CULBERTSON
President, Moody Bible Institute

October 1, 1959

Acknowledgments

Most pictures in this book are taken from the more than 4,000 photographs and other illustrations in Moodyana files. Some came from the Moody Bible Institute Promotion Department, the *Arch* (M.B.I. yearbook), Alumni Association, and former students, as well as the Chicago Historical Society, newspapers, and other sources outside the Institute, as indicated by credit lines.

We gratefully acknowledge permission from the following for use of copyrighted material:

The Curtis Publishing Company

William B. Eerdmans Publishing Company

The Rodeheaver Company

Delbert L. Hall

Wendell P. Loveless

For much invaluable background material, in chapter I especially, I am indebted to the McCormick Collection of the Wisconsin Historical Society in Madison, and to Mrs. Lucile Kellar, its co-ordinator. In this excellent collection of the papers of Mr. and Mrs. Cyrus H. McCormick and others in the family, I first learned many important details of developments in the Bible Work and the Chicago Evangelization Society during the crucial period of 1886-89. This is especially well recorded in the letters and reports of Miss Emma Dryer to Mrs. McCormick.

A special word of thanks is due Warner Sallman, whose beautiful art work on the jacket captures the thrilling story of D. L. Moody's prayer for a site for a school (see p. 27), as well as the tremendous growth from the very beginning to today's imposing LaSalle Street landmarks. Incidentally, Mr. Sallman's evening school attendance here in 1914 and 1916 was one significant factor in the production years later of his famous painting of the head of Christ, more than 100,000,000 prints of which have been distributed.

—BERNARD R. DEREMER

October 5, 1959

D. L. Moody

"Some day you will read in the papers that D. L. Moody, of East Northfield, is dead. Don't you believe a word of it! At that moment I shall be more alive than I am now. I shall have gone up higher, that is all; out of this old clay tenement into a house that is immortal—a body that death cannot touch, that sin cannot taint, a body fashioned like unto His glorious body.

"I was born of the flesh in 1837. I was born of the Spirit in 1855. That which is born of the flesh may die. That which is born of the Spirit will live forever."

So spoke the great nineteenth-century evangelist who founded Moody Bible Institute. Here is a brief chronological summary of important events in his life:

1837   Born February 5, East Northfield, Mass.

1854   Went to Boston to work.

1855   Led to Christ in shoe store, April 21, by his Sunday-school teacher, Edward Kimball.

1856   Arrived in Chicago, September 18; soon after began Sunday-school "recruiting."

1860   Gave up business for full-time Christian work.

1861-65   Served with U. S. Christian Commission during Civil War. (First delegate sent from Northwest Branch.)

1862   Married Emma C. Revell, sister of Fleming H. Revell, publisher, August 28.

1864   Illinois Street Independent Church (now Moody Church) organized.

1866   President of Chicago YMCA.

1867   First visit to Great Britain. Met Charles H. Spurgeon, George Mueller and others.

1870   Met Ira D. Sankey at YMCA convention in Indianapolis, and formed lifetime association with him.

1871   Chicago fire October 8, 9, destroying Moody's home and Illinois Street Church.

Moody's epochal experience of a new enduement of power by the Holy Spirit.

North Side Tabernacle (now Moody Church) dedicated December 24, replacing Illinois Street Church.

1872   Third visit to Great Britain, when he heard Evangelist Henry Varley say, "The world has yet to see what God will do with a man fully consecrated to Him." (This remark profoundly influenced D. L. Moody, and caused him to return the following year.)

1873-75   Fourth visit to Great Britain, and first great campaign. Moody-Sankey hymnbooks introduced.

1875-76   First great American campaigns, in Brooklyn, Philadelphia, New York and Chicago.

1876   Chicago Avenue Church (now Moody Church) dedicated.

For the remainder of his life, Moody was almost constantly engaged in evangelistic meetings, from one day to six months in length. Dr. R. E. Day, in *Bush Aglow*, estimated that Moody "spent almost 10,000 days and nights in meetings, which if put together would make a continuous revival more than 25 years long."

1879 Northfield Seminary (now Northfield School for Girls) opened.

1880 First of the annual Northfield summer conferences, which exerted a remarkable influence on the Bible conference movement.

1881 Mount Hermon (Mass.) School for Boys established.

1886-87 Preliminary steps toward organization and incorporation of Chicago Evangelization Society (now Moody Bible Institute).

1889 First structure for Chicago Evangelization Society (153 Institute Place) completed; school formally opened in its own building.

1893 May 7 to October 31, World's Fair evangelistic campaign, Chicago; nearly 2,000,000 total attendance.

1898 Chairman, evangelistic department, Army and Navy Christian Commission of YMCA during Spanish-American War.

1899 Became ill November 16, while conducting Kansas City campaign.
Died of heart dilation at home, East Northfield, Mass., December 22.
Funeral December 26, followed by memorial services in many leading cities all over America and Great Britain, and in other countries as well.

Outstanding Tributes to D. L. Moody . . .

"It is generally recognized that Mr. Moody spoke to more different people in the last quarter of the nineteenth century than any other man."
—DR. WILBUR M. SMITH

"You may take into consideration all the years of public services in this land and Great Britain, take into consideration all the addresses he delivered, and the audiences of his churches, and it will reach 100,000,000."
—DR. A. T. PIERSON, at Moody's funeral

A recent scholarly publication places this 1899 estimate "entirely within the realm of plausibility." In the October, 1957, *Quarterly Journal of Speech*, Dr. Rollin W. Quimby also says, "Certainly Moody would be a legitimate candidate for the title of 'most-listened-to-man-in-the-world' in the days before microphones."

"He deserves to be remembered as the greatest evangelist of his day, perhaps the greatest since John Wesley."
—Chicago *Tribune*, February 8, 1957

"He was absolutely simple and humble. In all the numberless hours I have spent with him, he never once manifested the least sign of affectation, never drew attention to himself, never alluded to the vast numbers that had attended his meetings, the distinguished persons who had confided their secrets to him, or the enterprises which had originated at his suggestion or been cradled under his care."
—F. B. MEYER

"He was greatest in his own home with his family, where Christ was first, others were second, and he was third."
—MAY WHITTLE MOODY, daughter-in-law of D. L. Moody

M. B. I. Leaders

DR. R. A. TORREY

1856-1928

A.B., B.D. Yale; studied abroad; saved at Yale, 1875; first personal work in D. L. Moody's New Haven campaign, 1878; ordained Congregational, 1878; pastorates in Ohio and Minneapolis; superintendent, MBI, 1889-1908 (on leave after 1901); laid groundwork for curriculum, especially Practical Christian Work program; pastor Moody Church, 1894-1906; world evangelistic tours, 1902-5, 1911, 1921—campaigns in many major cities of four continents; founded Montrose, Pa., Bible Conference, 1908; first dean, Bible Institute of Los Angeles, 1912-24; first pastor, Church of the Open Door, Los Angeles, 1915-24; author of more than 40 books, as well as many articles and tracts.

DR. JAMES M. GRAY

1851-1935

D.D., Bates College; LL.D., Des Moines University; rector, First Reformed Episcopal Church, Boston; lecturer on English Bible, Reformed Episcopal Theological Seminary, Philadelphia; one of the founders of the Sunday Protective League and Committee of One Hundred; pulpit supply, Clarendon Street Baptist Church, Boston; summer lecturer, MBI, from 1892 on; dean, 1904-23, president, 1923-34; president emeritus, 1934; supply pastor, Moody Church; consulting editor, Scofield Reference Bible; author of widely known synthetic plan of Bible study, as well as nearly 20 books, numerous articles, tracts and hymns; militant foe of theological liberalism.

DR. WILL H. HOUGHTON

1887-1947

Student, Eastern Nazarene College; D.D., Wheaton College; LL.D., Bob Jones University; began stage career in Boston; yielded his life to the Lord in Brooklyn; served with Dr. R. A. Torrey as song leader and singer at Montrose, Pa., Bible conference; pastorates in Pennsylvania; Baptist Tabernacle, Atlanta, Ga., 1925-30; Calvary Baptist Church, New York City, 1930-34; president, MBI, 1934-47.

DR. WILLIAM CULBERTSON

1905-

B.S., Temple University; B.D., D.D., Reformed Episcopal Theological Seminary, Philadelphia; LL.D., Bob Jones University; elected bishop of New York and Philadelphia synod of Reformed Episcopal Church when only 31 years old; rector three churches; dean of education, MBI, 1942-47; acting president, 1947; president, 1948; member, North American Council, China Inland Mission; chairman of advisory council, American Association for Jewish Evangelism; member, Scofield Bible revision committee; editor-in-chief, *Moody Monthly*; frequent contributor to other Christian periodicals in U.S.A. and Great Britain; speaker at English Keswick convention, as well as Bible conferences, churches, schools and other meetings.

R. A. TORREY

JAMES M. GRAY

WILL H. HOUGHTON

WILLIAM CULBERTSON

Original Trustees

NATHANIEL S. BOUTON

1828-1908

MBI trustee 1887-1890

Organizer and incorporator of the Union Foundry Works, Mr. Bouton was noted as "one of the most prominent producers of architectural iron and railway castings in the west." He had come to Chicago in 1852, and worked for a foundry, making car wheels and castings for the railroad industry then developing, of which Chicago was to become the center.

In 1857, Mayor Wentworth named Mr. Bouton Superintendent of Public Works, and it was during his administration that the first street paving in Chicago was done.

He was one of the 12 original members of Chicago Relief and Aid Society, which figured prominently after the great Chicago fire. His other interests included serving as president of the YMCA and the Chicago Bible Society. He was one of the organizers of the Kenwood Evangelical Church.

JOHN V. FARWELL

1825-1908

MBI trustee 1887-1908

Farwell was such a close friend, associate and supporter of Moody that he was called "the inventor of Dwight L. Moody." He countered with, "I didn't create Moody, God did."

A prominent dry goods merchant, he founded the John V. Farwell Co., which "ranked among the foremost business enterprises of Chicago." (The firm was bought out by Carson, Pirie, Scott & Co. in 1925.)

Farwell was the first superintendent of Moody Church Sunday school. He also served as vice-president of the Board of Trade; presidental elector on the Lincoln ticket in 1860; and member of the U. S. Christian Commission during the Civil War. Later he became Indian Commissioner during President Grant's administration.

He donated his first residence lot in Chicago to the YMCA for its original building (Farwell Hall), where many of the early Chicago Evangelization Society classes and meetings were held. Under one of the provisions of his will, a certain amount was set aside in trust establishing the "Moody Evangelist Fund," in order to "perpetuate the name of Moody in connection with the work he loved so well." It was to be used for the living expenses of men selected by MBI to hold evangelistic meetings throughout the country. The limited income from this fund is still being used by the Extension Department.

NATHANIEL S. BOUTON

JOHN V. FARWELL

T. W. HARVEY

ELBRIDGE G. KEITH

CYRUS H. McCORMICK, Jr.

ROBERT S. SCOTT

T. W. HARVEY

1835-1909

MBI trustee and vice-president, 1887-1893

Founder of the lumber company bearing his name, Mr. Harvey was "one of Chicago's pioneer lumbermen and at one time the greatest retail lumber dealer in the world." In 1878 he built in Michigan the first logging railroad ever constructed to transport logs from the camps to the streams and mills. He also introduced high-speed machinery in his lumber shops.

He also founded the town of Harvey, 20 miles south of the Chicago Loop, and was director of the Metropolitan National Bank and president of the YMCA. For 26 years he was Sunday-school superintendent of the Wabash Avenue Methodist Episcopal and Second Presbyterian Churches. Mr. Harvey was the first vice-president of MBI, as well as chairman of the executive committee for erection of the Chicago Avenue Church (now Moody Memorial Church), and director of the Chicago Relief and Aid Society, which was especially prominent after the great Chicago fire.

Mrs. Harvey was the first chairman of the ladies' advisory board of MBI.

ELBRIDGE G. KEITH

1840-1905

MBI trustee and treasurer, 1887-1905

A native of Vermont, Mr. Keith early settled in Chicago. He was one of the organizers and president of the Metropolitan National Bank here, and later became president of the Chicago Title and Trust Co.

A few of his many other activities included serving as a member of the Chicago Board of Education; trustee of Beloit (Wis.) College; president of the YMCA; and treasurer of the Chicago Bible Society.

Keith Hall in the old MBI Auditorium (formerly Moody Church) was named for him. The public elementary school at 3400 South Dearborn Street, Chicago, erected in 1883, also bears his name.

CYRUS H. McCORMICK, JR.

1859-1936

MBI trustee 1887-1893

Son of the famous inventor of the reaper (who was also a friend of D. L. Moody and supporter of his work), Mr. McCormick served at various times as president, chairman of the board, director, and executive committee member of the International Harvester Co. During the 33 years he headed the organization, he pioneered in an organized safety movement, voluntary compensation for workers injured on the job, and company pensions.

Rated one of the wealthiest men in the country, he was a large benefactor of many organizations. He gave the present YWCA building, 1001 North Dearborn Street, in memory of his first wife, Harriet Hammond McCormick.

He also served as a member of the special diplomatic mission to Russia in 1917, was a trustee of Princeton University, and a director of McCormick Theological Seminary.

Both the elder and the younger Mrs. Cyrus H. McCormicks were members of the ladies' advisory board of the women's department in the early days of M.B.I.

ROBERT S. SCOTT

1838-1904

MBI trustee 1887-1900

A native of Ireland, Mr. Scott came to Illinois in 1856, the same year D. L. Moody arrived in Chicago. He settled in Amboy, and became a salesman in a dry goods firm. In 1865 he moved to Chicago and went into partnership with Carson, Pirie, and Co., giving the firm its present name. At the time of his death, he was its senior partner.

He was a member of the Union League Club and of the First Presbyterian Church of Evanston.

CH. 1 *I have laid the foundation*

I Cor. 3:10

D. L. MOODY
1886-1899

A huge crowd thronged Farwell Hall, the downtown Chicago YMCA building, on Friday noon, January 22, 1886. On this cold, windy, snowy day, D. L. Moody was to speak on "city evangelization." Business and professional men, ministers, mission workers, and women had assembled to hear the great evangelist.

After a spirited song service, the bearded, gray-haired, heavy-set veteran rose to speak. He pointed out that some 25 years before, he had given up business to devote his life to evangelism. He was tremendously concerned about reaching the masses in the great cities, especially Chicago, so many of whom never went to church, and he urged upon his hearers the importance of a plan to have churches open every night, send out visitors, and raise up an army of volunteers to "act between the preachers and the people."

But central to all this was the requirement that this corps of workers "should be taught the Word of God so they could answer every question put to them."

"You are doing well," he said, "but we must *push* it." Push it—a characteristic and favorite phrase of dynamic D. L. Moody, who was forever pushing men and movements with all his boundless energy.

The Farwell Hall meeting was a birth pang of what is today Moody Bible Institute, oldest institution of its kind in the world, and model for some 200 other similar schools.

The complete history of M.B.I. has never been written. The natural place to begin is at the beginning, which, strangely enough, is somewhat lost in obscurity. Those who want to know who taught the *very first* class, where it met, how many attended and who they were, are doomed to disappointment.

Implicit in the origin of M.B.I. is the life and work of Miss Emma Dryer, whose important ministry in this connection seems largely unknown today. So, at long last, let us bring her out of the shadows into her rightful place.

For several years, Miss Dryer had served as principal and teacher at Illinois State Normal University. One summer day in 1870, not long after coming to Chicago, she met D. L. Moody through mutual friends. The following year, after the great Chicago fire, she was for a time YWCA secretary, ministering to the needs of the thousands of homeless people without food and clothing. At the same time, she was developing a program of Bible study, teaching and home visitation, a solid foundation for her later life and service. Through the North Side Tabernacle,[1] Miss Dryer, still associated for a time with the YWCA, carried on an ever widening ministry.

[1] A few weeks after the fire destroyed the Illinois Street Church (the first building ever erected for Moody's work) he built the North Side Tabernacle, at Ontario and Wells Streets, which was used from 1871-73. It was replaced by the Chicago Avenue Church in 1874. These buildings were forerunners of today's Moody Memorial Church at Clark Street and North Avenue.

Farwell Hall

North Side Tabernacle, said to be the first public structure erected for religious and educational purposes on the north side after the Chicago fire; later a public school

As early as 1873, she and others urged upon Moody the founding of a permanent school to train Christian lay workers. He clearly foresaw the need and possibilities of such an institution; however, in a sense, Miss Dryer was too late. By now Moody was outgrowing Chicago. His first great campaign, 1873-75, in the British Isles skyrocketed him to national and international fame, and it became apparent that he could no longer expect to return to permanent residence in Chicago. (Immediately after the 1871 fire, he had moved his family back to Northfield, Mass., his boyhood home.)

Never formally ordained, he was now "evangelist-at-large." The Sunday school and church he had founded years earlier were now

Miss Emma Dryer

Chicago Avenue Church, 1887
Courtesy Chicago Historical Society

well established. In 1876 their new building, the Chicago Avenue Church, was dedicated, and the second full-time pastor, Dr. William J. Erdman, was called.

Meanwhile, Miss Dryer's full-time "Bible Work," as it became known, was flourishing, supported financially by Mrs. Cyrus H. McCormick and others. After the fire, Miss Dryer and a faithful corps of volunteers carried on daily mothers' meetings averaging about 300, and children's industrial schools averaging about 400. And Miss Dryer reported, "The Bible was taught in them all." By 1878, there was an incorporated group, the Bible Work of Chicago, with classes meeting in Farwell Hall.

One of Miss Dryer's early reports gives this interesting glimpse into a fruitful ministry:

> In this visiting, we work more slowly than does the ordinary canvasser; for we invite people to meetings, children to Sunday school, and to sewing school and to day school[2]; we try to induce people to read the Bible and *we re-visit* many to help them in the study of the Scriptures. We sell Bibles on partial payments, and are glad to call many times to gather the small sums and to read the Bible with the purchaser; we extemporize meetings with adults or children,

Mrs. Cyrus H. McCormick, 1885. This great philanthropist was then 50.

Courtesy Chicago Historical Society

and hold Children's Meetings in which we teach them a simple catechism whose answers are texts of Scripture.

At that time, workers were serving in three areas of the city: north, west, and south.

As time went on, a home at 100 Warren Avenue (now 1713 Warren Avenue) was secured for Miss Dryer's work. There the women she selected lived, worked, studied, and went out to various parts of Chicago with the Gospel.

D. L. Moody never forgot the need for an enlarged and expanded work in Chicago which would include provision for training men, a permanent school, adequate buildings and staff. But after his return from Europe the demands

Dr. W. G. Moorehead, president
Xenia (U.P.) Theological Seminary

[2] Educational opportunities and facilities then were, of course, vastly different from today's. "In 1870-71 . . . slightly over one half of those enrolled (in Chicago public schools) availed themselves of the opportunity. . . . Many parents made no pretense of sending children to school at all." Dr. Bessie Louise Pierce, *A History of Chicago 1848-1871;* New York: Alfred A. Knopf, 1940, Vol. II, p. 391. Copyright by the University of Chicago.

had been great: huge campaigns in Brooklyn, Philadelphia, New York City and elsewhere. After the founding of his schools and conferences at his Northfield, Mass., home (1879-81), the demands upon him were even greater to maintain, support and promote these mushrooming enterprises.

As the conviction grew in Chicago that a larger, better organized and more permanent work was needed, weekly prayer meetings in Farwell Hall began to be devoted to this purpose. On Saturday mornings W. E. Blackstone, Fleming H. Revell, Miss Dryer and others met to pray. About 1883, Dr. C. A. Blanchard, president of Wheaton College and supply pastor of the Chicago Avenue Church, raised the money to call Dr. W. G. Moorehead, president of Xenia (U. P.) Theological Seminary, for a "test" institute—Bible classes of several weeks' duration.

Finally, as a result of the 1886 Farwell Hall meeting described before, Cyrus H. McCormick, Jr., subscribed $100,000 and others lesser amounts toward a program of city evangelization, including a formal training school.

From the vantage point of nearly the three-quarter-century mark in the history of the Bible institute movement, it is hard to imagine the situation when there was *no* such organization anywhere! In those days of pioneering, no pattern existed for the embryonic school struggling to be born. A later *Institute Tie* (now *Moody Monthly*) editorial tribute (September, 1900, p. 1) to D. L. Moody said:

> There was no school in the wide world that opened its doors to the class of men and women he wanted to train; nor was there any school that offered the kind of training that he proposed to give.

On the day he was 50 years old, February 5, 1887, D. L. Moody and a group of others met in his room in the Grand Pacific Hotel in downtown Chicago. A new organization, the Chicago Evangelization Society, was formed

that day, and soon after Miss Dryer's work was merged with it.

But it was far from smooth sailing ahead. Many problems of organization and administration had to be worked out. Since D. L. Moody lived a thousand miles away and was not often in Chicago, much had to be settled by correspondence. With the rapid growth of his work at Northfield, it was doubtless a great strain and burden to undertake such an additional responsibility as the Bible institute.

Yet later in 1887, he said, "I have never had my heart so set on anything as on this society" (C.E.S.). But certain difficulties were insurmountable, and finally it was necessary to separate Miss Dryer's Bible work from the C.E.S., though for a time she remained on the board of managers[3] of the latter. Later, she carried on an extensive program of home visitation and Bible distribution under the auspices of the Chicago Bible Society.

The years 1886-88 were marked by difficulties of many kinds. Bitter labor battles, typical of the times, had culminated in the terrible Haymarket Riot of 1886. It was hard to collect the money pledged to the C.E.S., partly because of economic conditions, partly because the local board was not satisfied with the arrangements for carrying on the work in Moody's absence. Sometimes it looked as if that long-awaited, greatly needed, and much-prayed-for school never would be realized!

Meanwhile under C.E.S. auspices, some 700 services were held in tents and missions, and 20,000 families were visited, mostly "those not attending regular preaching anywhere." This was carried on largely under the supervision of Merton Smith, an evangelist and associate of D. L. Moody.

Yellowing files reveal thrilling stories of Gospel triumphs in those early days. One sum-

---

[3] This group of 15 persons, mostly businessmen, pastors, and wives, included six of the original incorporators and trustees listed on pages 18-20. From the very beginning, the board of trustees has been the top governing body.

It seems that the board of managers developed into the "Ladies' Advisory Board of the Women's Department," which was discontinued about 1906.

CERTIFICATE FOR CORPORATIONS NOT FOR PECUNIARY PROFIT. Form No. 606. Printed by the Chicago Legal News Co.

2
4922

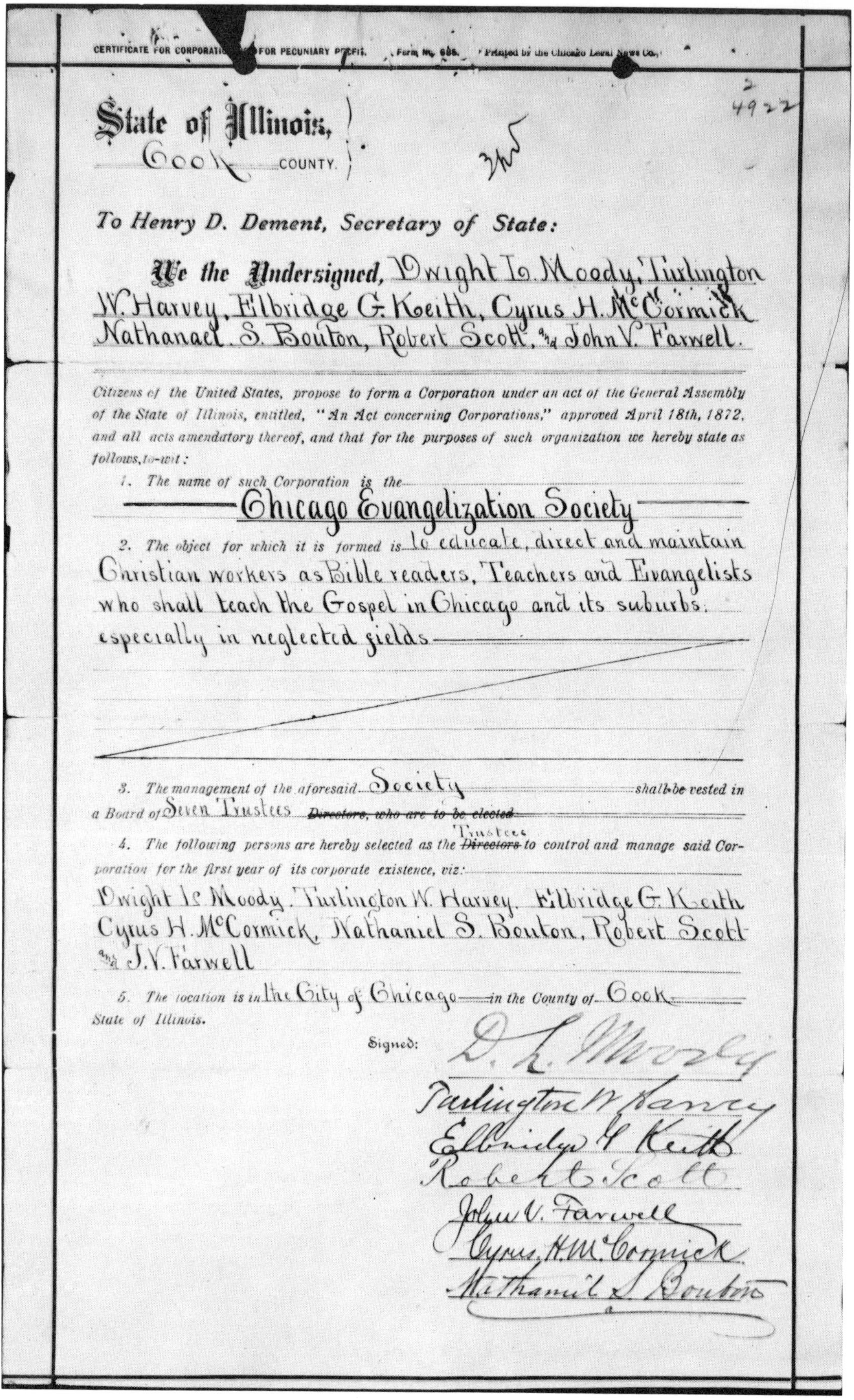

State of Illinois,
Cook COUNTY.

To Henry D. Dement, Secretary of State:

We the Undersigned, Dwight L. Moody, Turlington W. Harvey, Elbridge G. Keith, Cyrus H. McCormick Nathanael S. Bouton, Robert Scott, and John V. Farwell.

Citizens of the United States, propose to form a Corporation under an act of the General Assembly of the State of Illinois, entitled, "An Act concerning Corporations," approved April 18th, 1872, and all acts amendatory thereof, and that for the purposes of such organization we hereby state as follows, to-wit:

1. The name of such Corporation is the Chicago Evangelization Society

2. The object for which it is formed is to educate, direct and maintain Christian workers as Bible readers, Teachers and Evangelists who shall teach the Gospel in Chicago and its suburbs: especially in neglected fields

3. The management of the aforesaid Society shall be vested in a Board of Seven Trustees ~~Directors, who are to be elected~~

4. The following persons are hereby selected as the Trustees ~~Directors~~ to control and manage said Corporation for the first year of its corporate existence, viz:

Dwight L. Moody, Turlington W. Harvey, Elbridge G. Keith, Cyrus H. McCormick, Nathaniel S. Bouton, Robert Scott and J. V. Farwell

5. The location is in the City of Chicago in the County of Cook State of Illinois.

Signed: D. L. Moody
Turlington W. Harvey
Elbridge G. Keith
Robert Scott
John V. Farwell
Cyrus H. McCormick
Nathaniel S. Bouton

Copy of incorporation papers, February 12, 1887, C.E.S. (now M. B. I.). Original documents on file in Springfield.

mer a tent was located at Crosby and Division Streets, on the north side, in an area popularly known as "little hell."

At first saloon-keepers were naturally antagonistic to the work. One of them hired a brass band to play in his saloon, the windows of which overlooked the tent. Two nights later, during the opening hymn, a messenger from the saloon quietly entered the tent, his head bowed, and a look of shame upon his face. He asked, "Could you sing softly tonight? My brother's little boy was run over about two hours ago and he is dying, and the noise frightens him as he wakes from unconsciousness. The little boy won't last long and I thought I'd come and ask you to sing low."

A hush of holy silence came over the audience as prayer was offered for the boy. Then one of the workers left with the man to give what help she could to the distressed family.

From that hour all opposition ceased, and the Gospel had free course in "little hell."

From 1,000 to 1,500 persons came to the meetings nightly, and personal workers visited nearly 2,000 homes in the needy area.

During this time, a series of two- or three-week "institutes" was held in which various teachers expounded the Scriptures and gave lessons in practical personal work. Dr. Moorehead, Dr. E. P. Goodwin and others taught Bible doctrine, elementary church history and "sermons and sermonizing" to "train young men and women for Christian work and to employ able Christian workers to teach the Gospel in Chicago and its suburbs." But the need for a building for the new C.E.S. was rapidly becoming more acute.

One evening when D. L. Moody was to preach in the Chicago Avenue Church, an usher, John Morrison, was checking doors prior to the service. Stepping outside the northwest corner of the building, he was arrested by, "Is that you, Morrison?" in Moody's deep booming voice. Moody went on to say, "Do

Tent meetings were an important early ministry of C. E. S.

you see that lot? Let us pray the Lord to give it to us for a school." (Moody's amazing prophetic vision!) After a short earnest prayer, they went back inside; . Moody to preach, Morrison to usher, and both to await a fulfillment of their petition. Even in the light of Ephesians 3:20, neither could have imagined the magnificent Moody Bible Institute plant of today, built up around that very lot!

Finally, 1889 saw plans for the largest and most elaborate institute to date. D. L. Moody himself was to be here for it; sessions were to meet in the Chicago Avenue Church. From San Francisco, he wrote on February 2, 1889:

> I see you have got the training school advertised now I want you to get it in to all the papers you can & let it go the length and breth of the countery & say if men and women will give a little time to training they can find plenty of fields to work in & let it be known that all can come and the teaching will be something like the confrence at Northfield but let it be pushed now for all it is worth.[4]

And it *was* pushed! At the opening session, on April 4, a prayer service was held at 9 A.M.; the convention proper opened at 10 with the hymn, "My Jesus I Love Thee." F. G. Ensign, C.E.S. secretary, explained the purpose of the convention, and Rev. William W. Johnson, of Brooklyn, delivered the opening address on the nature of inspiration and methods of Bible study.

When D. L. Moody, just returned from the Pacific coast, came to the platform, he was delighted to find some 500 in attendance, where he had expected perhaps 100! In his opening remarks, he said, "Now we want to avoid all formalities—let us spend about an hour shak-

ing hands and getting acquainted with each other. Tell us what you are here for, what you hope to accomplish."

In his first address that day, Moody declared, "Word and work is the keynote of this convention. God sent you here. Every man and woman has a work to do, even in eternity. You must do your work or it will be left undone."

He went on to stress the necessity for raising up co-workers for ministers who will "stand with them and help them." Three-fourths of the inhabitants of the city went to no church, he declared, and therefore must be visited in their homes by trained workers. The great need was for trained laymen, "gap" men, as he often put it, to fill the gap between clergy and people. He noted that many times

F. G. Ensign

ministers seemed to be educated "away from the people," and warned that the minister "should not be invisible six days in the week and incomprehensible on the Sabbath."

Afternoons and evenings were given to visitation and mission work. When the session closed, May 10, 1889, after a period of great interest and enthusiasm, Moody promised that meetings would be held at 10:30 A.M. daily in the church and in tents in three districts all summer long; and "Lord willing I'll be back

[4] D. L. Moody's own formal education was quite limited, perhaps ending at the fifth grade, because of a combination of factors including the early death of his father. However, his poor grammar probably resulted as much from haste as from any other factor. With his tremendous zeal and drive to accomplish great results, he did not take time to write legibly, spell words correctly and construct proper sentences. See original letters and sermon notes on display in Moodyana.

Annie Rosie, early student, and later matron for many years

Mrs. Sarah B. Capron, first superintendent of women, 1889-94

Hugh H. McGranahan, first director of music

in September and we'll have another conference."

Within a month, the board of trustees had bought the property at 228-32 LaSalle Avenue (three houses next to the Chicago Avenue Church), and the Judge Anthony property on West Pearson Street, the lot for which Moody and Morrison had prayed. Remodeling of the three adjacent houses was rushed, and almost immediately construction was begun on a three-story men's dormitory and main office building at 80 West Pearson Street. In only a few short years of amazing growth (and after Chicago's new uniform street-numbering system), that structure was to become known around the world as 153 Institute Place, the building that named a street, and in a very real sense marked the beginning of the entire Bible-institute movement.

Casting around for someone to head up the infant school, Moody picked as superintendent brilliant young Dr. R. A. Torrey, graduate of Yale College and Seminary, who had also studied abroad. (Moody's own formal schooling was woefully lacking, but there was nothing wrong with his insight!) Torrey had gotten his first taste of soul-winning in Moody's great New Haven campaign on the threshold of Yale University. Noticing the young theological student attending night after night, Moody told him, dramatically, "Young man, you'd better get to work for God!" Little did D. L. Moody know the mighty forces he was unleashing in thus stirring R. A. Torrey to service—and how this was to be bread cast on the waters a decade later.

Rich from revival atmosphere which had characterized his ministry in pastoral and city mission work, Dr. Torrey arrived on September 26, 1889. This was the formal opening in its own building, after years of prayer and preparation, of the Bible Institute of the Chicago Evangelization Society. Miss Annie Rosie, one of the very first students (Sept. '89-Oct. '91), recalled that the original full-time staff numbered exactly six: Dr. Torrey; Mrs. Sarah B. Capron, superintendent of women; Miss Gertrude Hulbert, her assistant; Mrs. M. L. Harper, matron; H. H. McGranahan, director of music; and George Sanborn, business manager. She also said, "At the first few meals in the women's dining room, the speakers, officers and three or four women students sat at one table, Mrs. Capron at the head and Mr. Moody at the foot."

Headquarters of the women's department was at 232 LaSalle Avenue (now about 818 North LaSalle Street, part of Crowell Hall).

Here were rooms for about 50 students, as well as dining room, kitchen, pantry and laundry.

The men's building was not quite ready for occupancy, but applicants were told they could board near the church for $5.00 to $7.00 a week until the dormitory was completed. Board in the Institute was $3.50 a week, in those long-ago, pre-inflation days; tuition was, of course, free. Non-residents who wanted to take the lectures without registering could do so for $5.00 a week. Students could "begin any time"; previously there had been apparently no formal registration, and it was "come when you can, leave when you must," with naturally a great turnover.[5]

The next milestone was January 16, 1890, the formal dedication of the 153 building. D. L. Moody outlined the purpose of the school to include training of women for city visitation and foreign missions, as well as men to become musicians and evangelists. Later, in a lengthy newspaper interview, he outlined something of his philosophy of education. Asked what studies would be pursued in the new training school, he replied:

> Mainly three. First I shall aim to have given a sufficient knowledge of the English Bible; so far as may be, a practical mastery of it. Second, I would have workers trained in everything that will give them access practically to the souls of the people, especially the neglected classes. Third, I would give a

[5] The first registered woman student, according to Central Records, was Mary E. Craven, who attended from Sept. 1889 to Oct. 1890; the first man, William Lagerquist, Oct. 1889 to Nov. 1890. (Both are deceased.) There are also incomplete records of a few transients who attended classes earlier in 1889.

First women's dormitories

Staircase, women's building

Dedication of 153 building, first structure erected especially for M.B.I.

Dr. Torrey teaching in Lecture Room

great prominence to the study of music, both vocal and instrumental. I believe that music is one of the most powerful agents for good or for evil.

It was carefully explained, many times, that this was no short-cut to the ministry, no substitute for college or seminary. However, those already in some form of Christian work, or preparing for it, were invited to the Institute to profit by some practical training which could probably not be obtained elsewhere.

D. L. Moody's own heavy responsibilities with the Northfield schools and conferences, and meetings around the country, prevented him from being here much. But, as Miss Rosie recalled, "It was an occasion of rejoicing on the part of the students when his coming was announced." When Mr. Moody was here, she said, he frequently took charge of classes. "He would not lecture us but talked in a fatherly way about practical things. He told the students to make 'rest day' different from every other day, to put away books—no studying to be done. . . . He told the men students not

to try to preach like someone else but to maintain their own individuality. He also told them not to lie on the pulpit when preaching but to stand erect and keep their hands out of their pockets."

Reception room 153 building. Business offices occupied these rooms later. This is now part of the Audio Visual Center.

William Evans

But Moody had to depend on Dr. Torrey and others in residence to carry on the daily instruction in the classroom and supervise the work of the students. To Dr. Torrey must go the credit for laying the groundwork for the curriculum, especially in the Practical Christian Work program.

For the first full year's work (1890), Dr. Torrey submitted this report to Mr. Moody:

	Men	Women
Total number enrolled	173	80
Church and mission meetings conducted	2,688	
Mission, cottage, and mothers' meetings conducted		258
Children's meetings conducted		434
Inquirers dealt with	9,405	2,376
Inquirers professing conversion	2,143	586
Visits made	7,243	15,523

In the music department, 578 persons were enrolled for vocal classes, and for private lessons, both vocal and instrumental. Music lessons given totaled 2,678. Men came from 31 states and nine foreign countries, some of them ministers and evangelists seeking further study.[6]

The very first graduate was William Evans, later the famous author and Bible teacher, who received his diploma in 1892. (There was no semblance of formal graduation exercises until 1905.) His story may be selected as typical of that of many early students.

As a young man who had come to this country only recently, he heard D. L. Moody in the Fifth Avenue Presbyterian Church, New York City. Evans recalled how forcefully Moody spoke from Luke 5 on the subject "Surrender all to Jesus Christ," and then appealing for young men to give their lives for His service, he looked down at Evans and announced abruptly, "Young man, I mean you." (There's that insight again!)

After the meeting, Moody said, "Young man, somehow or other God told me He meant you. Have you never been called to give your life to the service of Jesus Christ?" Evans, then a young convert, was a typesetter for the New York *World* "and getting a comfortable salary," but he had also given weeks of anxious thought to the ministry, and had been helping in mission work.

"I knew what it meant, giving up my position and salary," Dr. Evans recalled, "and a life of self-denial for sometime to come, and I was not willing. After I had gotten my breath, I said, ' I don't know. I have been thinking about it.' 'Well,' he said, 'you go, and prepare yourself for Christian work.' The lady who was with me said, 'He hasn't any money.' 'Did I say anything about money? Young man, you pack up your trunk and go to my school in Chicago.' I said, 'I can't go. I haven't enough

[6] Condensed from complete report in *Record of Christian Work,* January, 1891, p. 3. By comparison, for a recent year, students (day, evening, and summer) reported a total of 53,939 persons dealt with; 3,910 professed conversions; 1,110 backsliders restored; 16,020 Bibles and Scripture portions, and 214,044 tracts distributed, according to Mr. James F. Harrison, director of Practical Christian Work.

Men students, 1890. The one at the right holding the horn is William Evans, first M.B.I. graduate

Women students of 1890, in front of their buildings on LaSalle Street

money to pay my fare.' 'Never mind money. Where do you live? Who do you work with?' "

Moody was a man of action, and the result was that in four or five days Evans was on his way to Chicago, with Moody's promise ringing in his ears, "Never mind about money. If God has called you, He will take care of you."

"When I got here," Dr. Evans went on, "I called at the office and found there was an allowance of $25.00 a month for me during my stay here. But through playing a cornet at the Pacific Garden Mission, I was offered work there playing at $5.00 a week, so I wrote them not to send me any more money as I was earning my way."

But later, it looked for a time as if Moody might have made a mistake. After Dr. Evans had been here awhile, he felt that he ought to have attended Mount Hermon School for Boys, the private secondary school near Northfield, Mass., which D. L. Moody had also founded. This was arranged, but after only a

Perhaps this was the 1893 version of "Heavy heavy hangs over thy head." The men apparently were members of the Ariel quartette: Will C. Gamble, '94, John Henry Boose, Ralph T. Fulton, and Carl B. Norlin, who was Institute cashier for many years.

short time Evans realized that he was wrong, and he should have stayed at the Institute!

Alas, this time Mr. Moody was not so sympathetic or receptive. In fact, he at first forbade Evans to attend the Institute. But Dr. Torrey interceded, and Evans was reinstated. By now he had learned his lesson on vacillation well. He said to Mr. Moody, "I will stay in Chicago, if I die in the Institute, until I get your signature on my diploma." When the honored number one diploma was received, he took it to Moody (perhaps as much as to say, "I told you so"), and asked, "Do you remember Northfield?" He said, "I do, but you needed it awfully bad." (Evidently this referred to a conversation in Northfield when Moody had rather bluntly told the young man to quit school and go back to work.) Evans was destined to become a faculty member here and a widely known and greatly used Bible teacher and author.

The World's Fair of 1893 brought a tremendously challenging opportunity to the vigorous young Institute. Characteristically, Moody had foreseen the influx of countless thousands to Chicago, so in 1892 the top two stories were added to the 153 building (as it is today) to accommodate visitors and increasing enrollment. Disregarding the doctor's warning to "slow down," D. L. Moody set to work planning the largest single campaign he ever conducted, in some respects! As Dr. Day points out in *Bush Aglow,* "There was a curious circumstance in the World's Fair Gospel Campaign: Moody was never, in any meeting of Chicago ministers or laymen, appointed or asked to head up the work! He was so obvious that such a formality was unnecessary. His years of specialized training, world-wide acquaintance with great men, universal love and confidence, unique and powerful local organizations, made his leadership so obvious that no one ever thought of passing a resolution." Moody himself used to say, "We don't want committees. When you want anything done, tell Mr. So-and-So to do it and you will accomplish something. If there had been a committee appointed, Noah's ark would never have been built."

A few statistics are staggering. Total attendance registered at the Fair on the far south side was more than 27,000,000. Moody's meetings drew—nearly 2,000,000!

This was perhaps the greatest clinic ever presented for personal work: meetings in some 80 different churches, tents, theaters, missions and halls all over Chicago, with foreign language services and other special features. And headquarters for this great endeavor was the 153 building. There workers reported nightly to D. L. Moody in his second-floor rooms, and each received some word of encouragement.

The Institute had been conceived and born in prayer, and each unfolding day held many answers. Surely one of the most remarkable ones in the early days occurred during the World's Fair Campaign. One day Moody, Torrey, and others met in Room 9 of the 153 building for counsel before the noon meal. Moody said, "I needed $7,000 for the work today. I have already received $1,000; let us kneel down and ask God to send us that $6,000." And in that childlike manner so typical of him, he prayed something like this (as recalled later by Dr. Torrey): "Heavenly Father, we need $6,000 right now to meet our honest obligations. Send us that $6,000 today."

During the meal and discussion that followed, a telegram was delivered to the room and immediately read aloud to the group: "D. L. Moody: Your friends at Northfield had a feeling you needed some money for your work in Chicago; we have just passed the baskets and there are $6,000 in the baskets and more to follow. (Signed) H. M. Moore, Boston."

Just as the morning session of the Northfield conference was closing that day, Dr. A. J. Gordon felt led to ask for that special offering. "And so," Dr. Torrey said, "a thousand miles away, at just a little after the prayer had gone up, as nearly as we could figure it, 3,000

Dormitory room, 153 building, about 1900

people put into the baskets the exact sum that Mr. Moody had asked for a few moments before in prayer"!

The work of the Institute grew and prospered. D. L. Moody was tireless in his efforts to raise funds for this work. The McCormicks and many others responded constantly and generously to his appeals, which were often scrawled in his own large bold hand. He also was constantly on the lookout for the best teachers, new methods, new opportunities for service.

In fact, because of his personal appeal and wide acquaintance, it could be said by 1900 that the Institute had been visited by almost every well-known Bible teacher who had been in America since its founding. They came to "give the best results of their Bible study and practice." Even a partial list looks like a top-flight *Who's Who* of the Christian world: F. B. Meyer, W. G. Moorehead, G. Campbell Morgan, Andrew Murray, A. T. Pierson, C. I. Scofield, J. Hudson Taylor, Prebendary H. W. Webb-Peploe and many others.

By the end of the century, the Bible Institute had completed its first full decade of work, exhibiting an amazing vitality. It looked forward under God to greater things; but its first great loss, and most severe testing, occurred at that time.

CH. 2 | *Preach the Word*

II Tim. 4:2

R. A. TORREY
1889-1908

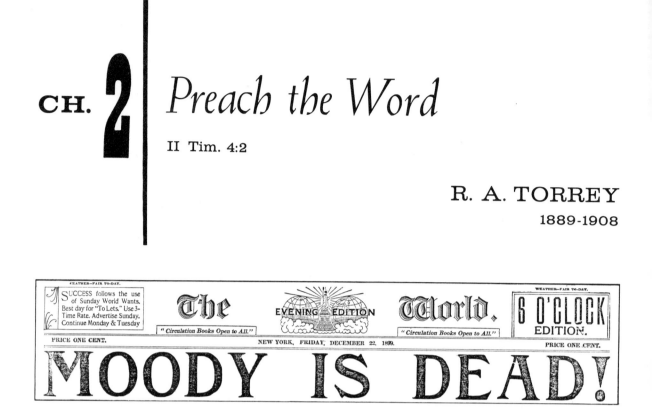

SUCCESS follows the use of Sunday World Wants. Best day for "To Lets." Use 3-Time Rate. Advertise Sunday. Continue Monday & Tuesday

The EVENING EDITION World. 6 O'CLOCK EDITION.

"*Circulation Books Open to All.*"   "*Circulation Books Open to All.*"

PRICE ONE CENT.   NEW YORK, FRIDAY, DECEMBER 22, 1899.   PRICE ONE CENT.

MOODY IS DEAD!

This screaming banner headline of the New York *World* evening edition, December 22, 1899, was only one of thousands of news items recording the departure of the great evangelist "to be with Christ, which is far better." Secular and religious papers alike attempted to chronicle the tremendous impact of his life and ministry. The Chicago *Times-Herald* took half of page 1, and all of page 2, on December 23, for this. Editorially, it said, "The greatest evangelist of the century has passed away"; similar tributes were legion.

Gloom at once settled over the Institute when news of the founder's death became known. The one who had been a friend and spiritual father to so many of faculty, staff and student body would be missed as few Christian workers have been missed. Torrey and many others had suffered a great personal loss. Among the hundreds of letters, telegrams and other messages that poured in upon the family was a handwritten expression of sympathy signed by 237 Institute students.

Nevertheless, Dr. Torrey predicted, "Though

Mr. Moody was the president and the leading spirit of the Bible Institute, our work will go on just the same . . . ." At its next meeting, the trustees voted in loving memory to change the name of the Chicago Evangelization Society to "The Moody Bible Institute of Chicago." (It had been constantly, though unofficially, called by Moody's name, but when it was proposed to link his name with any of his institutions, he used to say, "Not as long as I am alive.") The scope of the work was also enlarged because of increasing demands and opportunities; not only Chicago and suburbs, but now the entire world was to be the field of labor of those trained here.

D. L. Moody had possessed great vision, energy and zeal, but had been able at the same time to delegate responsibility and work. At the time of his death, the Institute was governed by a board of seven trustees. Soon afterward, A. P. Fitt, Moody's only son-in-law, was elected to the board. (William H. Holden, a brother-in-law of Moody, was one of the attorneys who handled legal matters in con-

36

nection with the change of name. Fleming H. Revell, another brother-in-law, became a trustee in 1900.)

On his deathbed, Moody had bequeathed the schools in Northfield to his older son, Will; the school in Chicago to Fitt. For many years, Mr. Fitt served on the board of trustees. For a number of those years, he was full-time secretary here, carrying the major responsibility in a rapidly growing work. (For a short time, he had the title of president.) He taught some, but was mostly occupied with administrative and executive functions in personnel, financial and educational matters. He prepared for the board of trustees the detailed annual reports of the Institute's work. In addition, he edited the *Institute Tie* (now *Moody Monthly*), *and* served as superintendent of the Bible Institute Colportage Association (now Moody Press).

Nevertheless, the years immediately following Moody's death were a difficult time of adjustment. The number one fund-raiser was gone. Others must attempt to take his place: securing finances, settling broad administrative problems, overseeing business details, guiding educational plans and programs.

About this time, the Institute's greatest benefactor, in many respects, appeared on the scene: Henry Parsons Crowell, later president and chairman of the board of Quaker Oats Company. Led into a deeper Christian life through the ministry of William R. Newell, assistant superintendent of M. B. I., Mr. Crowell was elected to the board of trustees in 1901, became president in 1904. For 40 years he held this high office, giving of himself, his time and his means to the work of M. B. I., in addition to other philanthropies. He attended executive committee meetings, usually held weekly, in which the vital decisions were made that shaped Institute policies and guided its course. (Dr. Gray used to say, "It was the brains and heart of H. P. Crowell that brought this institution up, that made this Institute." [1])

Other great men were attracted to the board of trustees, such as Dr. Howard A. Kelly of Baltimore, the world-famous surgeon and gynecologist. William Whiting Borden, scion of a wealthy family, and immortalized as missionary enthusiast "Borden of Yale," was perhaps the youngest man ever elected to the board. Upon his death at 25, Princeton Semi-

A. P. Fitt

Will R. Moody

Henry Parsons Crowell   William R. Newell   Dr. Howard A. Kelly

nary said, "Probably in the history of the Christian church, no man of his years has ever provided so largely for the evangelization of the world." Practically the whole of his fortune, approximately $1,000,000, was bequeathed to missions; M. B. I. received $100,000. (Contrary to a popular idea, he was not related to the Borden milk family; his father was a lawyer, but his grandfather had made the fortune in Chicago real estate.)

About this time another name appeared on the roster of the board: Thomas S. Smith, apple king of the Midwest, and father of Dr. Wilbur M. Smith. A young man of 21, he walked forward in the Chicago Avenue Church one night when D. L. Moody was preaching. The great evangelist took his hand, looked in his face, and said, "Young man, God has a place for you!" (That insight again!) Sixty years later, Mr. Smith could repeat the very words!

For 43 years this quiet, unassuming businessman held membership on the board, serving as vice-chairman for more than 20 years. Many M. B. I. graduating classes over the years remember his godly counsel to preach the Word and live the Word. His own example of arising at 4 A. M. daily, in order to have

adequate time for Bible study and prayer before going to the old South Water Street market, inspired all who knew him.

Dr. Gray, brought here by D. L. Moody as a summer lecturer for a number of years, entered upon his full-time permanent responsibilities in 1904, as dean. The number one graduate, William Evans, accepted a call in 1903 as faculty member, and within a few years became director of the Bible course. As the Institute grew, J. H. Todd became the first superintendent of men. A. F. Gaylord, a student in 1891, became business manager later that same year. For 44 years he held that

A. F. Gaylord

[1] Dr. R. E. Day, *A Christian in Big Business* (the life story of Henry Parsons Crowell), Moody Press, 1954, p. 174.

William Whiting Borden   Thomas S. Smith   James H. Todd

office, supervising buildings, maintenance, personnel, accounting and legal matters.[2]

One of D. L. Moody's principal objects was to "give a great prominence to the study of music, both vocal and instrumental." Unable to carry a tune himself, he always recognized the great power of Gospel music. Early in his career, he enlisted Ira D. Sankey, the pioneer of evangelistic singers, for a lifetime association. However, it was Hugh H. McGranahan, nephew of the famous composer James McGranahan, who first headed the M.B.I. Music Department. The first year, 2,678 music lessons were given, testifying to its immediate and overwhelming success.

McGranahan was succeeded by Dr. D. B. Towner in 1893, who did most in the early days to build up the Music Department. E. O. Sellers said, "Taken as an all-around . . . teacher, conductor, soloist, composer and author, D. B. Towner doubtless had no equal; certainly none exceeded him. Others of course equalled him or perhaps excelled him along one or more of these lines, but none could equal him in a combination of them all." Other early associates were W. C. Coffin, teacher of voice, and Edward Howells, teacher of piano, cabinet and pipe organ. Classes met

Dr. D. B. Towner, in his office, 153 building

Edward Howells

[2] Of course, as M. B. I. grew over the years, some of these responsibilities were either shared with or turned over to other individuals and offices.

Women's dining room, on LaSalle Street

Men's dining room, first floor 153 building

in the 153 building, and also in the Chicago Avenue Church, utilizing its fine pipe organ built by Kimball about 1894.

Let's go back to the turn of the century and take a look at a typical day in the life of an M.B.I. student. The rising bell is at 6:45, except on Sunday and Monday; breakfast bell at 7:30. (Now it's rise at 6, breakfast at 7.) Devotions followed the meal. Of course, there were separate dining rooms then; men ate in the 153 building, women in the dining room of their buildings on LaSalle Street next to the Chicago Avenue Church.

Monday was rest day—no classes. This was the occasion for picnic lunches in the park, boat rides on Lake Michigan, or ice skating or sledding in Lincoln Park, according to the season. A tennis court on Clark Street near Newberry Library was a favorite spot for some.

This was a typical schedule for the rest of the week:

M.B.I. students, 1898. Newberry Library in background

Tuesday

9:00 A.M.	Chapter Summary
10:00 A.M.	Elementary Notation
11:00 A.M.	Personal Work, or Report Hour
2:30 P.M.	Male Chorus
5:00 P.M.	Physical Culture
8:00 P.M.	Synthetic Bible Study

Wednesday

9:00 A.M.	Normal Bible Class
10:00 A.M.	General Chorus
11:00 A.M.	Bible Doctrine
1:30 P.M.	Elementary Harmony
5:00 P.M.	Physical Culture

Thursday

9:00 A.M.	Methods of Children's Work
10:00 A.M.	Advanced Notation
11:00 A.M.	Bible Doctrine
1:30 P.M.	Advanced Harmony
5:00 P.M.	Physical Culture

Friday

9:00 A.M.	Missionary Study and Prayer Union
10:00 A.M.	Elementary Notation
11:00 A.M.	Bible Doctrine
1:30 P.M.	Normal Training Class (Music)
5:00 P.M.	Physical Culture

Saturday

9:00 A.M.	Analysis of Romans
10:00 A.M.	Conducting Class
11:00 A.M.	International Sunday School Lesson
5:00 P.M.	Physical Culture

Twelve hours' study a week was expected, and each student had five "appointments" (assignments) weekly. The object of the Practical Work course was "to test students, as well as train them. Many do not know the gift that is in them until they are put on trial." Students would help in church and evangelistic services, city and rescue missions, Sunday-school classes, women's and children's meetings, open-air meetings, home, hospital and jail visitation.

In one of the earliest notices, D. L. Moody had said, "I have felt that more personal work must be done by men and women who were trained for it." The Practical Christian Work program soon became an outstanding and distinctive feature of the Bible Institute. About

Above. Open air meeting, 1912, about 555 South State Street

Left. Jail visitation

1902, an article in a British Isles publication said, "The idea of the Gospel wagon probably originated at the [Moody] Institute, but has become so popular that it is now seen in nearly all of the large cities of the U. S. and some in Europe." These wagons, containing a small organ, a desk for a pulpit, and several students, were driven through various parts of the city. Here and there the wagons would stop, and meetings fifteen or twenty minutes long would be held. In this way, thousands were reached with the Gospel message who seldom or never saw the inside of a church.

But there were more prosaic tasks too. Each student was required to do an hour's domestic

Gospel wagons in front of 153 building

work daily (or "dum" work, as it was called). Mrs. J. T. Wade (Grace A. Van Duyn, Dec. '09) recalled that her first job was washing glasses and silver after breakfast, and at other times dusting offices. She found that the hour's work could be done in fifteen or twenty minutes if one were fast and efficient enough![3]

"Prompt as the stroke of 6 o'clock was the evening tea-bell," recalled Margaret Blake Robinson, former newspaperwoman and author of *A Reporter at Moody's* (1900). "We have chicken and ice cream for dinner. Every former student knows it is Wednesday, for that is the day the brown hen comes down from her perch in the family coop to gladden the student's heart." Afterward, the "evening Bible talk," a delightful tradition, was followed by "dum" work, visiting in the parlor, studies or assignment to close the day.

Another great institution was the report hour, first at 11 A.M. Tuesday, later 9 A.M. Students gave reports on their assignments, received instructions and suggestions as to difficulties.

Friday at 9 A.M. the Missionary Study and Prayer Union met. Through the inspiration of missionaries on furlough, many life decisions for the foreign field were made in these meetings. This was the predecessor of Missionary Union, which has fostered and promoted missionary interest through the years—in praying, giving and going.

The first Tuesday morning of each month a prayer hour for both faculty and students was held. These meetings helped to foster the family feeling, especially as the student enrollment grew. Upon occasion, such as a financial crisis, all classes would be suspended, and faculty and students would spend an entire day in prayer. Of course, many other regular prayer meetings were held, besides the daily morning and evening devotions: dormitory, dining room and assignment groups. The only prayer meeting for men and women students together was held before breakfast Sunday in the library of the men's building. On Saturday night, prayer and testimony meetings were held.

Other special features in the early days included "verse day" for the girls. Mrs. Wade recalled that each Thursday, after the noon

[3] Because of the very small staff in the early days, students had to do many of the household duties. This practice continued until about the time of World War II.

Library, first floor 153 building

meal, all would go to the parlor of the Women's Building and stand around the room. The superintendent of women would stand behind the parlor table, quote a verse, then the girls would all repeat it after her, kneel down, and someone would lead in prayer.

Volumes could be written of God's faithfulness in answered prayer in the lives of students with many and varied needs. One of the greatest, of course, has always been financial. In those early days, even the modest sums needed (board and room was $3.50 a week) were not always easily obtained. Many a student has gone through on Philippians 4:19 and faith, when cold cash was in short supply.

One day Mrs. Wade was looking at Bibles in the bookstore, her own being about worn out. She decided to pray for one costing $2.50, although she preferred a $4.50 one. No one else knew of this need, except another student who

This scene of Victorian elegance was the office of Miss Charlotte A. Cary, assistant superintendent of women 1898-1908; superintendent 1908-23.

one day whispered to her before class, "I am praying for a Bible." Mrs. Wade replied, "So am I." Not long afterward, an anonymous package was delivered to Mrs. Wade: the $4.50 Bible! There was no clue as to the donor; the package had been left by a small boy unknown to the girl answering the door at the Women's Building.

From the earliest days, students have had the experience of going to the post office and finding an envelope containing money from "a friend." Sometimes it would be the exact amount for a particular need.

Deepening of the spiritual life was the inevitable result of being brought under the ministry of the Word of God, the teaching of the classroom, application in the dormitory, on assignments, and in all other phases of life.

One outstanding chapter in the history of M.B.I. is that of Founder's Week. Undoubtedly the outstanding winter Bible conference of the Midwest, it began in a small way. Popular tradition has it that the origin of Founder's Week was D. L. Moody dashing into a classroom (or the dining room) and declaring, "It's my birthday; let's go for a sleigh ride."

The earliest official notice is in the *Institute Tie* (now *Moody Monthly*) of February, 1901, then edited by Mr. Fitt: "A new day for annual observance has been decided upon by the faculty—Feb. 5th, Mr. Moody's birthday—Founder's Day. While Mr. Moody was with us, it was his custom to outvote the whole faculty of the Northfield schools, and give a general holiday in both institutions on his

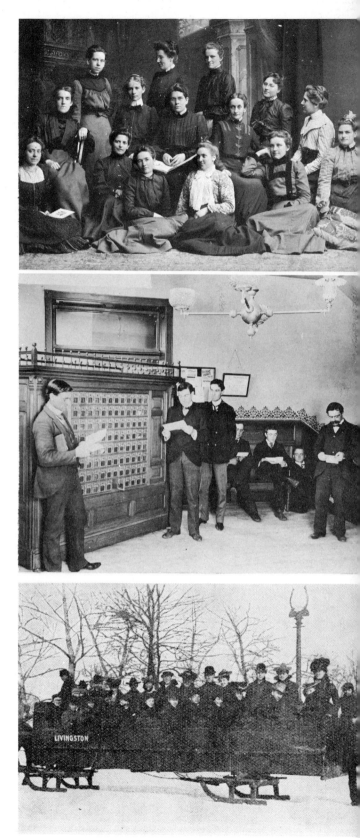

Miss Cary with a group of students. Seated at extreme left is Miss Annie Rosie, early student, later matron for more than 40 years. When she retired, it was said that she "was known and loved by more former students, doubtless, than any other individual in the history of the Institute."

Post office, second floor 153 building, about 1900. Mail from home was good news then too, especially when it contained some folding money!

Founder's Day sleigh ride, about 1905

birthday. Some of the most playful and kindly reminiscences about him cluster around these anniversaries. While the Institute has not usually observed the occasion in similar fashion, the faculty have now inaugurated this memorial movement, and beginning with Tuesday, Feb. 5th, of this year, the day will be observed with special exercises."

For several years, February 5 was observed as Founder's Day, with a holiday from classes, or a day of prayer, recollections of D. L. Moody, and illustrated lectures on his life and work. Sleigh rides did occur, at least in 1904 and 1907. An evening social time was also held in Moody Church on occasion.

In 1911, for the first time, a week-long observance occurred marking the 25th anniversary of M.B.I. Regular classes met in the morning, while afternoons were given over to "receptions and symposiums from 2 to 5, and popular meetings in the church in the evenings."

The next week-long meeting was a "revival conference" in 1917, from January 31 to February 5, marking the 30th annual reunion of M.B.I., and the 80th anniversary of D. L. Moody's birth. Week-long conferences were also held in 1919, and from 1921-24. A *Moody Bible Institute Monthly* article in March, 1926, declared, "Founder's Week Reaches Its Majority—a Survey of the 21st Annual Conference." We still follow the same anachronism today.

But the conference has brought together outstanding Bible teachers for a time of rich ministry, looked forward to annually by students, staff, former students and other visitors. Reunions of former students have always been a most enjoyable and blessed time of the entire week.

Second midwinter conference, Chicago Avenue Church, January 3, 1907

Founder's Day meeting in Lecture Room, February 5, 1914

James M Gray
1935.

©D.L.Hall

Dr. Gray at lake front, 1935

CH. 3 *Contend for the faith*

Jude 3

JAMES M. GRAY
1904-1935

It is interesting and challenging to observe how, in M.B.I. leadership over the years, the mantle of Elijah has more than once fallen upon a ready Elisha. In 1892, D. L. Moody first brought Dr. James M. Gray here as a summer lecturer. Thereafter, he was almost continuously associated with this work in some way for more than 40 years. In 1904, he became the first dean.[1] After Dr. Torrey left, Dr. Gray was the top administrative officer, although he did not receive the title of president until 1923.

Perhaps Dr. Gray is chiefly remembered as author of the synthetic plan of Bible study. This valuable supplement to analysis and other methods means simply the study of the Bible as a whole, and each book as a whole, as well as in its relation to the other books. "Synthesis," as the late Dr. Harold L. Lundquist used to say, "raises questions but doesn't answer them." As thousands of former students can testify, this method has done more than anything else to give a comprehensive view of the Book of books.

Dr. Gray's gifted pen was early recognized by D. L. Moody, who frequently asked him to write articles for various papers. One letter

from Moody to Dr. Gray closed, ". . . and I hope you will use your pen." Later, as author and editor of the Institute magazine, Dr. Gray exerted a wide influence through his ministry of writing.

Perhaps nothing reveals more clearly Dr. Gray's deep spirituality and humility than this quotation from a letter which Betty Scott (later Mrs. John Stam) wrote her father, a missionary in China, during her first term at M.B.I.:

> Dr. Gray did not wait for me to make myself known, but fairly early in the fall sent me a nice note asking if I could come to his office at a certain hour. How charming and lovable a man he is! I just love him! And he inspires me with awe. More than any other person I ever heard, he gives the sure impression of "speaking with authority," like the old prophets. Yet nobody could ever accuse him of being conceited. He surely is a spiritual-minded man. It was worth coming to Moody just to meet him, I think.

Though quiet and dignified, Dr. Gray was capable of an amazing amount of humor. In taking an offering, or on other suitable occasions, he would often regale his hearers with a humorous story. His secretary for many years, Miss Clara Schlegel, recalls that on occasion she would hear a hearty laugh from his office. Later, when called in for dictation, she would learn the cause: some bitter, critical letter, often revealing a woeful ignorance of

---

[1] Originally the plan was to have three deans, Dr. Torrey, Dr. Gray, and probably Dr. Scofield. Each would give four months a year, one term, to teaching in the Institute, and eight months to Bible teaching or evangelism in the field. After Dr. Torrey left, the plan was abandoned. William M. Runyan, *Dr. Gray at Moody Bible Institute,* p. 139.

First graduating class—
November, 1905.
Left to right: front, Miss Jewel
Brandt, Mrs. Etta Bowman,
Miss F. E. Miller; rear, Pearl
H. Hughes, John F. Vonckx,
Harry E. Kiefer and John T.
Sharman

the facts. Instead of taking offense, Dr. Gray would laugh it off and say, "God pity the man who takes his work too seriously."

Dr. Gray had been fond of swimming. But during his later years at the Institute, his chief diversions were daily walks to the lake and to his home at 29 East Division Street, as well as horseback rides in Lincoln Park.

A few of his aphorisms, never to be forgotten by his hearers:

"Push your work; don't let your work push you."

"I deny the allegation, and defy the alligator."

To students at exam time: "Do not ask the Lord to bring back to your mind that which never entered your mind!"

To tardy students: "You have an appointment with God; be here on time!"

A favorite verse, which he often used in autographing Bibles and photographs, was John 12:26: "If any man serve me, him will my Father honor." This promise was certainly fulfilled in his own life.

The graduation of seven students at one time from the rapidly growing school, in the early days of this century, marked such an unusual event that the picture here reproduced appeared on the *Institute Tie* (now *Moody*

Monthly) cover the following month. Each of these students "had completed the two years of residence, study and training, and had passed written and oral examinations, thereby earning the diploma of the Institute. Brief but pleasant graduation exercises were held at the 11 o'clock hour on November 1 when the diplomas were awarded by Dr. Gray." This was apparently the first semblance of formal graduation exercises.

Presumably the faculty, staff and students at M.B.I. have always been consecrated Christians, eager to know and do the will of God. Yet in this sacred atmosphere, Satan can bring in unholy influences, and there can be need for revival.

One of the most outstanding revival experiences occurred in October, 1906, as an outgrowth of Monday night prayer meetings in the 153 building. O. O. Wood, '07, recalled that when Dr. William Evans called on a student to lead in prayer one morning, it seemed to be like the beginning of any other class. But after only a few sentences of prayer, "the Holy Spirit came upon that body of students. Sobs and audible prayer came from all parts of the Lecture Room, and soon everyone was on his knees. Then began such a time of prayer, intercession and confession as many of us had

50

never seen before, and few have seen since."

Sins were confessed, restitutions were made, and human forgiveness sought and received. All classes were dismissed; there was no thought of the noon meal, and the revival continued the next day.

An editorial in the *Institute Tie* the following month declared that there was "little or no false fire or extravagance. A deep and abiding work of grace has been wrought in hearts, making it a time of, perhaps, more widespread individual cleansing and blessing than the Institute has ever known. To God be the thanks and glory!"

From time to time over the years, God has visited the Institute with an unusual outpouring of His Spirit. There have been other occasions when, a spiritual need having been felt, classes have been suspended for a special time of wait-ing upon God. All-night prayer meetings have likewise been held from time to time, sometimes by Institute officials, at other times by students on their own initiative.

From its small beginnings, M.B.I. grew amazingly. In 1904, there were eight buildings. Additional space was acquired in all directions to accommodate the rapidly increasing enrollment. The next construction was an additional men's dormitory at 152 Institute Place (now Norton Hall) in 1909, followed two years later by the Women's Building at 830 North LaSalle Street (now Smith Hall, a men's dormitory). This afforded for the first time a combined dining room, and made possible other changes. The library could now expand and take the entire west side of the first floor in the 153 building.

Other buildings were bought or rented, but

Dedication of land for men's dormitory, 152 Institute Place, May, 1909. Buildings in background faced Chestnut Street, part of present site of Torrey-Gray Auditorium. At the platform are, left to right: front, Dr. D. B. Towner and Dr. A. C. Dixon; seated at small organ, George S. Schuler; Dr. Gray, John Hunter, Dr. William Evans and Dr. Torrey.

On Alumni Day of Founder's Week in 1951, the building formally became Norton Hall.

Dedication of ground for Women's Building, 830 North LaSalle Street, August, 1910. At dedication of completed building, June 5, 1911, Henry Parsons Crowell, president of board of trustees, pointed out that enrollment in day and evening school totaled more than 900, and said, "We are all filled with hope that in the not too far distant future, we shall find, in the day department alone 1,000 students."

On Alumni Day of Founder's Week in 1951, the building was formally named Smith Hall.

the next milestone in the M.B.I. building program was the acquisition of the former Moody Church, after that organization had moved to the Tabernacle on North Avenue, part of the present site of Moody Memorial Church.[2] The historic building, in which many of the very first Institute classes had met, became the M.B.I. Auditorium in January, 1918.

From the earliest days, romance has been a factor in Institute life. Miss Rosie recalled

that a young student from Ireland became interested in a German girl. (Love knows no international boundary line.) Unfortunately, she "discouraged all his advances." The disappointed young man went to Mr. Moody (instrumental in bringing him here) and laid the matter before him. Our founder promptly sent for the girl, had a talk with her. Result: the couple soon became engaged, "and were married when they finished their course."

Although the popular 830 building was "no man's land," it became known as the "match factory." "Matches" were indeed made there; where better could one obtain a life's partner than at M.B.I., among the cream of the crop of Christian young people? Hundreds of

[2] In spite of a common founder, proximity, use of the same facilities, and close ties of fellowship, there has never been an organic connection between M. B. I. and Moody Church. However, some men have served on the boards of both organizations at the same time. In fact, Dr. Torrey was for several years pastor of the church and superintendent of M. B. I. concurrently.

Dining room, about 1912

Library, first floor, 153 building

M.B.I. faculty, 1911. Left to right, front row: J. H. Ralston, Miss A. M. Taylor, Miss C. A. Cary, Miss D. M. Sellers, William Norton; middle row, J. H. Hunter, H. W. Pope, J. M. Gray, D. B. Towner, William Evans, A. F. Gaylord; back row, J. B. Trowbridge, E. A. Marshall, E. O. Sellers, George S. Schuler, W. C. Coffin, W. L. Gilpin. Not shown are P. W. Campbell and C. P. Meeker.

couples met and in due time were wedded—sometimes in Massey Chapel.

M.B.I. has always been interdenominational. By 1912 some 40 denominations were represented among faculty and students. The Institute had been founded simply to "educate, direct, and maintain" Christian workers to "teach the Gospel." But in Dr. Gray's time the devastating inroads of Modernism became increasingly felt in the church at large. Proclamations from the University of Chicago, Andover-Newton, and other centers of Modernism (most of which had formerly been staunchly conservative) undoubtedly troubled and confused many. This was a day of trumpets giving "an uncertain sound"; many were not preparing for the battle as a result.

God's people must be rallied to proclaim and defend the "faith once delivered to the saints." M.B.I. must take its own distinctive place of leadership for the cause of Christ; it must become a foremost spokesman for evangelical Christianity.

And so this statement appeared in the 1915-16 catalog, "by direction of the trustees of the Institute as an expression of its doctrinal belief and the teaching of its classrooms":

The brethren gathered for the International Conference on the Prophetic Scriptures heartily endorse the declarations made by the previous prophetic conferences; but also feel it their solemn duty, in view of existing conditions in the professing church, to re-state and reaffirm their unswerving belief in

53

the following fundamental truths of our holy faith:

1. We believe that the Bible is the Word and Revelation of God and therefore our only authority.

2. We believe in the Deity of our Lord Jesus Christ, that He is very God by whom and for whom "all things were created."

3. We believe in His virgin birth, that He was conceived by the Holy Spirit and is therefore God manifested in the flesh.

4. We believe in salvation by divine sacrifice, that the Son of God gave "His life a ransom for many" and bore "our sins in His own body on the tree."

5. We believe in His physical resurrection from the dead and in His bodily presence at the right hand of God as our Priest and Advocate.

6. We believe in the universality, and heinousness of sin, and in salvation by Grace, "not of works lest any man should boast"; that Sonship with God is attained only by regeneration through the Holy Spirit and faith in Jesus Christ.

7. We believe in the Personality and Deity of the Holy Spirit, who came down upon earth on the day of Pentecost to indwell believers and to be the administrator in the church of the Lord Jesus Christ; Who is also here to "reprove the world of sin, and of righteousness, and of judgment."

8. We believe in the great commission which our Lord has given to His church to evangelize the world, and that this evangelization is the great mission of the church.

9. We believe in the second, visible and imminent coming of our Lord and Saviour Jesus Christ to establish His world-wide Kingdom on the earth.

10. We believe in a Heaven of eternal bliss for the righteous and in the conscious and eternal punishment of the wicked.

Furthermore, we exhort the people of God in all denominations to stand by these great truths, so much rejected in our days, and to contend earnestly for the faith which our God has, in His Holy Word, delivered unto the saints.

As it grew in prestige and power, M.B.I. became a citadel of the faith around the world. Pastors, former students, Christians generally asked: What does M.B.I. teach? What does it say concerning this particular matter?

Some religious leaders, of course, looked

During the Chapman-Alexander campaign, the evangelists and their associates visited M.B.I., October 29, 1910. After a tour of the buildings and lunch in the gym, the group left in these automobiles for the tabernacle erected for the north side meetings.

View is looking east on Institute Place. Note at extreme left the soft drink bottling works which stood where the Sweet Shop is now. B.I.C.A. bookstore and offices were on LaSalle Street, part of present site of Crowell Hall.

Early international character of M.B.I. is indicated by this group of British students in 1909.

Report Hour, Massey Chapel, September, 1916. Glass doors opened onto 830 lobby.

Dr. William Evans teaching in Lecture Room, April, 1913

Above—Assembled for the great Prophetic Bible Conference, of February 24-27, 1914, was a group of ministers "the like of which could not be gathered together today in the English world," according to Dr. Wilbur M. Smith. The conference was sponsored by M.B.I., with morning, afternoon and evening sessions in Moody Church. This photograph was taken at 10 A.M., Thursday, February 26.

Dr. Smith goes on to say that no other "gathering anywhere has left such an abiding impression upon me as that one of 1914. While the solemn messages and warnings of that conference were ridiculed in newspaper reports that week, today the ominous nature of the world crisis in which we are living compels our journalists to resort to the very apocalyptic vocabulary then decried as the result of pessimism, while the church as a whole seems so strangely silent on the great truths of the prophetic Word of God."

Left. Howard W. Pope, superintendent of men, in his office on second floor 153 building, 1913

askance at the Institute, but others were unstinting in their praise. Dr. Francis L. Patton, president of Princeton Theological Seminary, said:

I wish to express my deepening interest in the work of the Moody Bible Institute, an interest which increases the more I know about it. The Institute is doing a work of the deepest importance in the sphere of religious experience. Others may be raising questions as to how and where we got our Bible, and some may be seeking to reply to them. Blessed be God, there is one place where they read the Bible as the Word of God, and whose students, having first ascertained its contents, go forth doing their best to convey them to other men. May it live and prosper.

Dr. Charles G. Trumbull, distinguished editor of the *Sunday School Times,* commented after a visit here:

I do not know when I have left anywhere not my own home with such a feeling of genuine homesickness as was mine when I had to say good-by to the Moody Bible Institute in Chicago last week. I can indeed say in deep earnestness that it was the most wonderful and blessed two weeks that the Lord has privileged me to have. The fellowship with others in prayer and service was unspeakably rich, and that marvelous atmosphere of first century Christianity in which the Institute seems bathed goes beyond any community life with which I have ever before been personally allowed to come in touch.

Indeed, the Institute was to become a mecca for visitors. In 1916, the Baptist Young People's Union of America and Christian Endeavor conventions were held in the Coliseum in Chicago. Groups were assembled there and brought to M.B.I. in its Gospel autos, where guides took them on tour. D. L. Moody's room was a principal attraction, as it is today. Told

More than 50 soldiers (most of them wounded overseas) and nurses from Fort Sheridan visited M.B.I., May 23, 1919. The group toured the Institute, enjoyed dinner and supper, an auto ride in Lincoln Park, and two evening classes. Visit was planned by Hugh Cork, M.B.I. Army and Navy Secretary.

M.B.I. World War I honor roll lists 313 names, of whom 125 were in religious work. Seven were killed in action.

Top. Presentation of class picture was a feature of morning exercises in M.B.I. Auditorium. Note American flag, which covered picture until moment of unveiling. For both class and graduation exercises, women always wore white (April, August and December), men dark suits and white shirts, in the days before caps and gowns.

Center. "Dorm party on the sly"

Bottom. Junior-Senior parties in Keith Hall, M.B.I. Auditorium became a high light of the school term.

These three photos taken about 1925 by Harold R. Cook, '26, Recreation Club photographer

that there were six and one-half acres of floor space, a 15-year-old boy commented, "I have seen many things grown on a space of six acres, but none that gave the results of your institution."

By 1929 so many individuals and groups came to visit M.B.I. that the office of the host was designated. With reception room and office in the 153 building, and the help of an assistant, the host welcomed 2,287 visitors during 1929, showing them the Institute film, and conducting them on tour.[3]

M.B.I. was developing as a school. It had a school song, loved by thousands all over the world, written by Dr. Gray and Dr. Towner in 1909. (Incidentally, the Alumni Association recently bought the copyright on the "Christian Fellowship Song.") Of course, for many years "Great Is Thy Faithfulness" seems to have been a sort of unofficial school song. Once when it was announced, a new student whispered to her neighbor, "What number is it?" (in *Voice of Thanksgiving No. 4*). Shocked reply: "108 —it's 108 in every hymnbook!"

School song, colors, spirit, athletic program —none of these elements were lacking. The 152 building boasted a gym for indoor sports; Lincoln Park and other outdoor facilities were used for tennis, wiener roasts, ice skating, and other activities, many sponsored by the popular Recreation (Rec) Club, including at least two annual institutions: the Memorial Day and

[3] During 1958, a total of 6,026 visitors were conducted on Institute tours.

Building strong bodies for the Lord's
work. Gym class, 1925

Recreation Club skating party, Lincoln Park, January, 1927

Ingredients: smoke, hot dogs, rolls, mustard, fellowship. Mix
well for good time, such as that enjoyed on this 1925 outing.

Evening school cafeteria line, 1920

Evening school students ate a well-balanced meal for 25 cents in Emma Dryer Room of M.B.I. Auditorium.

Watermelons, cantaloupes, and other produce from Thomas S. Smith market, headed for M.B.I. kitchen. Scene is on Chestnut Street, north of 830 building. This stub end of Chestnut, vacated to M.B.I. by the city, July 8, 1931, is now part of Torrey-Gray Auditorium.

Fourth of July picnic outings. Early morning Thanksgiving Day football games also were enjoyed.

Concerning II Timothy 2:15, Dr. Torrey declared, "That text has been the motto of Moody Bible Institute from its beginning. I do not know who adopted it as the motto; but from the very first printed matter that went out from the Institute, that text stood at the top of it. The Institute has lived up to that text." [4]

A milestone for evening school occurred September 17, 1918, when its work was correlated with that of the day school. This meant that students in evening school could, for the first time, cover the same ground as day students, receive the same training, be awarded the same diplomas. To cover a regular course in evening school, it was necessary to spend four years of 37 weeks each. [5]

The staff at M.B.I. grew rapidly too. The original six had grown to nearly 300 by 1929. The Household Department, responsible for all housekeeping activities, always had a busy schedule, especially when serving 16 separate meals a day! These included 6:45 A. M. early "breakfast for the help," three other breakfasts, one lunch, five dinners (11:45 A. M. to 12:40 P. M.—the main meal was at noon then), six suppers (including evening school from 5:15 to 6:15, and one at 6:30 P. M. for students employed outside).

The Institute, a work of faith, has always depended on the free-will gifts of God's people for its existence. Tuition is free; board and room are provided to students approximately at cost. (Prior to World War I, students paid $4.00 a week room and board, provided they did one hour's work a day.)

Let's take another look at the daily schedule of a student and see the changes wrought in less than two decades. Miss Eva Milton, Aug. '18 graduate, presented in her address during class exercises this report of a student's daily life:

6:00 A.M.   Rising bell

[4] Address given February 5, 1911, reported in *Christian Workers Magazine* (now *Moody Monthly*), February, 1916.

[5] Evening school now offers two courses: basic Bible (no academic prerequisite), which can be completed in two years, leading to the certificate of recognition; and the general evening course (for high-school graduates), which contains 36 semester hours, offers four branches of specialization, and leads to a certificate of graduation.

6:35 A.M.   Quiet hour—private devotions

6:50 A.M.   Breakfast bell

7:00 A.M.   Breakfast, preceded by song of praise, and thanks returned by "one' of the men"

Morning devotions in Massey Chapel come next, followed by an hour's domestic work. This takes care of part of the week's board for the student, and enables the Household Department to operate with a minimum of hired help. All work around the buildings, except scrubbing and cooking, is done by students.

9:00 A.M.   School begins; 50-minute class periods until noon.[6]

12:20 P.M.   Assemble in dining room; grace sung or prayer offered.

[6] At this time, five basic courses of study were available. The same general schedule applied to the men, who met in the Lecture Room for devotions. All students spent 10 to 12 hours a week in Practical Christian Work assignments.

After a happy social time around the tables, several missionary prayer bands meet. Certain classes, such as manual arts, meet in the afternoon. Many students have employment.

5:30 P.M.   Supper

6:00 P.M.   Evening devotions in Massey Chapel

6:30 P.M.   Those going on assignments meet in the gym for prayer and conference. Every day except Monday "our students are proclaiming the Gospel of Jesus Christ in every corner of the city."

Others may enjoy a social time, a walk to the lake, or other diversion.

7:30 - 9:00 P.M.   Study hours

9:00 - 9:30 P.M.   Visiting time in the corridors

9:30 P.M.   Quiet time

10:00 P.M.   Lights out—"day is done"

Hebrew class, 1923, in what was then said to be the "only Jewish missions course in the world." In center background is Nathan J. Stone, first graduate of the course, behind the instructor, Solomon Birnbaum.

CLASS IN HOME NURSING

Home nursing class, 1925

Chapter summary class in Keith Hall, 1932, taught by Clarence H. Benson

Open air meeting, September, 1919, Maxwell Street

Practical Christian Work assignment at Municipal
Tuberculosis Sanitarium, 1922

Former students looking back on Institute days are always thankful to God for many things, not the least of which is their Practical Christian Work assignments. Yet, for many, it wasn't easy at the time. Some students who came to M.B.I. had never visited or done personal work before. Many dreaded certain assignments, and some girls were unable to start out without a good cry beforehand (and one of relief and release afterward!).

Some knew a measure of persecution, especially open-air groups in certain neighborhoods when stones, eggs or tomatoes were hurled at them. Sometimes the air was let out of the tires on the buses.

But through all these experiences, students found that "He is faithful," and they grew in grace and in knowledge of Him. Countless numbers will be in glory because of the work of M.B.I. students on assignments over the years; and this while the students themselves

Students singing and bringing
Bible message to Cook County
Jail prisoners

were laying a foundation for a lifetime of ministry in the Word of God.

From D. L. Moody's petition for the ground on which the 153 building stands, prayer has always been an integral part of M.B.I. life. During this period, there was a prescribed quiet time for private daily devotions. In addition, many regular gatherings were given at least in part to prayer: devotions after breakfast and supper, Missionary Union prayer bands, floor prayer meetings weekly in each dormitory. Then the entire Institute family—faculty, staff, and students—met for prayer Saturdays at 8:30 A. M., as well as 9 A. M. on the first Tuesday of each month.

In fact, a *Moody Monthly* editorial said that on an average more than 1,300 regularly scheduled prayer meetings were held a month, besides numerous spontaneous gatherings in dormitories, offices and classrooms. This mighty volume, coupled with the intercession of faithful prayer warriors around the world, is the force that sustains this place! Reams

could be used in writing of thrilling answers to prayer in every area of life. Another result is the testimony of visitors that they can feel the power and presence of the Lord here. When Henry W. Frost visited the Institute in 1908, he wrote in the guest register, "Surely, the Lord is in this place!" Here students have formed lifetime devotional habits, and for many prayer has become a greater reality than ever before.

The earliest music offices and studios had been housed in the all-purpose 153 building. The first building used exclusively for the Music Department was on the east side of North LaSalle at 831. (Crossing LaSalle Street in those halcyon days was hardly the life-and-death matter it is with today's heavy volume of fast traffic!) In the fall of 1924, the Music Department was located in its building at 835 North Wells Street (formerly a rooming house), said to be "the first of its kind in the country"; that is, devoted exclusively to teaching Gospel singing and playing. Anyone who

65

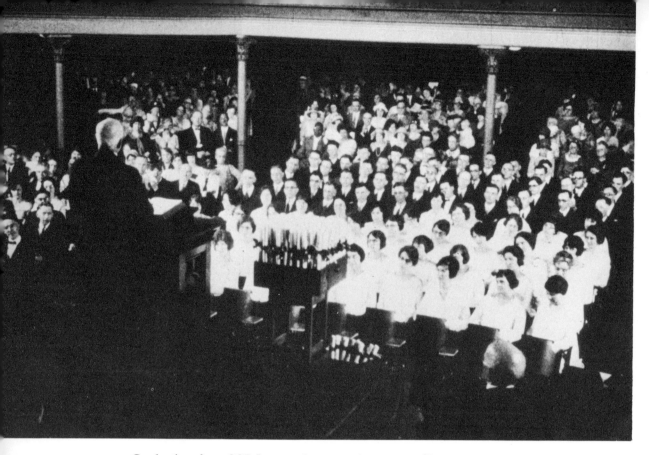

Graduation from M.B.I. was always an important milestone. Note diplomas, rolled for presentation, on table and floor of platform in Auditorium. This was probably August, 1925, class.

Diplomas being awarded by Henry Parsons Crowell, president board of trustees. Distaff note: Miss Jackson wears a cloche-type hat, popular in the 1920's.

Evening fellowship meeting, Lecture Room, 1925

M.B.I. faculty, 1927

Oh, what an ordeal it was to lead singing in one of "Bitty's" classes! But, he *trained song leaders!*

ever lived in Ransom Hall or other nearby dormitories can never forget the sound of dozens of students going up and down the scales, both vocal and instrumental, especially in warm weather with all windows open! And on Tuesday and Friday nights! The four-story building, costing some $50,000, housed offices, pipe organ, studios, and practice rooms.

For many years, the Auditorium Choir was directed by Talmage J. Bittikofer, of the music faculty. At Founder's Week and graduation, this choir was always heard, as well as on occasion over WMBI, or in special renditions of "The Creation," "The Holy City," and similar works.

The possibility of reaching the masses with the Gospel by an entirely new medium—radio —gripped the hearts of several at M.B.I., in-

cluding young Henry Coleman Crowell (son of Henry Parsons Crowell), assistant to the president. From 1923 on, he and others were praying for such an opportunity. At first, special programs were broadcast over stations WGES and WENR. Then, a 500-watt transmitter was bought from WWJ, Detroit, and installed at M.B.I. But no wave length could be obtained! The group continued to pray, and finally an unused channel became available. On July 28, 1926, WMBI went on the air, broadcasting from a studio in the 152 building and a control room and transmitter on top of the 830 (North LaSalle) building!

From the first, there was no doubt as to the Lord's leading and blessing, in the eager response of delighted listeners, including many who were saved through the programs. Mr.

Genial George Schuler giving
organ lesson in Recital Hall
No. 1 of Music Building, 1925

Auditorium Choir, October, 1928, directed by Talmage J. Bittikofer; Organist Alfred Holzworth

On the second floor of the 830 building, low French doors opened out upon a flower-bordered roof garden, pleasant setting for leisure moments. It was used at least once for a junior-senior party.

Reception Hall, Women's Building, 1925

LaSalle Street looking south from Chestnut, 1925, with Women's Building in foreground

LaSalle Street looking north from Chicago Avenue, 1927. First WMBI transmitter was in penthouse on top of 830 building. Antenna was stretched between towers shown on top of 153 and 830 buildings.

Original WMBI studio, 1927, first floor 152 building. Left to right: William E. King, Alfred Holzworth, Mrs. T. J. Bittikofer, Wendell P. Loveless, Mrs. Myrtle Raedeke Comfield, Miss Gladys Mary Talbot, Mr. Bittikofer

The triumvirate that directed M.B.I. affairs: executive committee of board of trustees, 1925. Left to right: Henry P. Crowell, Dr. Gray, Thomas S. Smith. Dr. Gray's office is now part of Moodyana exhibit.

James W. Davis, superintendent of men, in his office on second floor 153 building, with Paul Arnold, Aug. '31

Jobs didn't grow on trees during the depression. These students were waiting for good news from the employment bureau, second floor, 153 building, in March, 1932. F. N. Burkey, in charge of the office, is seated in background.

Crowell, admirably suited by his natural abilities and training at Yale University's Sheffield Scientific School, became the station director. Other milestones were to follow: 1928, the new 5,000-watt transmitter at Addison, Ill. (in use today); the "midnight hour" program, actually heard in such faraway places as India; a full daytime schedule in 1941; and use of United Press news wire service the same year.

Institute personnel were heard on other stations too, as broadcast experience and opportunities grew. On July 7, 1935, the WMBI Gospel singers (or "Moody Institute Singers") made their debut on a special NBC network for a weekly series. Mr. Bittikofer was director, Wendell P. Loveless narrator. Dr. Gray spoke on WGN and other Chicago area stations on occasion.

And so, as the Institute approached the half-century mark, it continued to grow and prosper under Dr. Gray's capable leadership. But he couldn't go on forever. Eventually there must be a successor; who would it be?

WILL H. HOUGHTON
1934-1947

"Dr. Gray, you have kept the faith!"

These thrilling and challenging words opened another great chapter in the history of M.B.I. On November 1, 1934, Dr. Will H. Houghton became president, and Dr. Gray president emeritus. At a formal inauguration service on November 9, Dr. Gray told of his desire for several years to pass the reins of administration "into younger hands while I was still here to counsel and co-operate with him." The trustees and Dr. Gray had finally settled on Dr. Houghton as the divine choice for this high office.

Dr. Houghton's address began with the words quoted above. He recalled that when he was a boy, his mother had told him of the work of D. L. Moody, and had expressed the conviction that sometime, somewhere, he would bear a relationship to that work! His first official act was to issue a call to prayer for God's continued blessing upon the Institute, and he suggested Friday, January 18, 1935, for groups of alumni and friends to gather for special intercession.

What did Dr. Houghton receive from Dr. Gray? An institution that had grown from fewer than 300 students to a day school of more than 900; an evening school of more than 1,000; a Correspondence School averaging 10,000; a plant that had expanded from eight buildings to nearly 40; vigorous Radio and Extension Departments; and a magazine reaching readers around the world—all enjoying the rich blessing of God.

A month after Dr. Houghton's inauguration, the entire Christian world was shocked by the martyrdom of John and Betty Stam, Apr. '32 and Apr. '31. (The effect was very much like that of the slaying of five young men by the Aucas in 1956.) On December 7, 1934, communist bandits ruthlessly looted their mission station at Tsingteh, Anhwei Province, China, taking them hostage and demanding $20,000. Before negotiations could be completed, their decapitated bodies were found along the road the next day.

At M.B.I. the news of these young martyrs challenged numerous students to offer their lives for foreign missionary service, and the story continues to inspire succeeding generations, especially through Mrs. Howard Taylor's *The Triumph of John and Betty Stam.* In loving memory of them, Dr. Houghton wrote a poem, "By Life or By Death," (see page 96) which was later set to music by George S. Schuler. It likewise has been widely used, and is a constant reminder of their devotion and sacrifice.[1] Incidentally, their infant daughter,

[1] To date 17 former students have been foreign missionary martyrs. First was Miss Ella Schenck, '96, killed May 4, 1898, in Africa. Most recent was Ancel Allen, '56, shot down in Mexico while dropping Gospels of John for Air Mail from God Mission.

While none of the five men in Ecuador were former students, one widow, Marilou (Hobolth) McCully is a graduate (Dec. '49).

Above. President Houghton in his new office, 153 building, now part of Moodyana exhibit

Right. Dr. Houghton (center) at his inauguration, with Dr. Gray (left) and Mr. Crowell

John and Betty Stam
Photo courtesy of China Inland Mission

Helen Priscilla miraculously escaped unhurt. She is now preparing for foreign missionary service.

Dr. Houghton early saw the tremendous possibilities for stimulating evangelism and revival by holding a great two-year celebration in 1936-37: the 50th anniversary of M.B.I. and centennial of D. L. Moody's birth. With characteristic vigor, he planned, worked, and set others to work toward this goal.

The years 1936-37 witnessed great meetings all over the United States and the British Isles sponsored by M.B.I. Speakers included Dr. Houghton, Dr. H. A. Ironside, Mel Trotter, Bishop J. Taylor Smith, and many others. Rallies and conferences were held in Royal Albert Hall, London; Carnegie Hall, New York City; and some 75 other cities. In fact, 2,300 churches from every state in the union

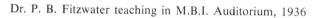

Dr. P. B. Fitzwater teaching in M.B.I. Auditorium, 1936

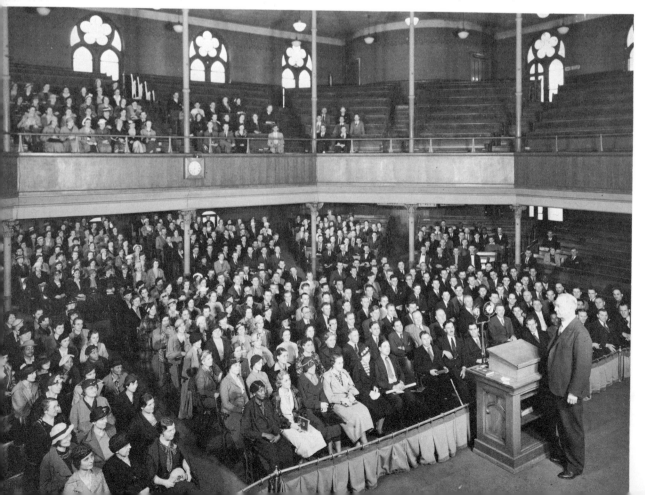

Metropolitan Opera House, Philadelphia, January, 1937

Display in Ayers Department Store, Indianapolis

This great crowd of 12,000 in the Chicago Coliseum paid tribute to D. L. Moody on the 100th anniversary of his birth (to the very day), February 5, 1937. Dr. Houghton

presided; principal address was by Bishop J. Taylor Smith, former chaplain general of the British Army.

Arrival of Bishop J. Taylor Smith, Union Station, Chicago, January 30, 1937

and 30 foreign lands observed "Moody Day," on Sunday, February 7, 1937, with appropriate programs. Many conversions were reported, with quickening of believers, and in some instances revival. "In this country," says Dr. Wilbur M. Smith, no one "related in any way to Christian work has ever had a centenary as widely observed and extensively commented upon as Dwight L. Moody." And one is tempted to question, has *anyone,* except a few national leaders such as Abraham Lincoln, ever been so honored on the 100th anniversary of his birth? Great metropolitan newspapers, like the Chicago *Tribune,* New York *Times* and others devoted as much as an entire page to reviewing D. L. Moody's life and work. Periodicals such as the *Christian,* the *Sunday School Times* and many others published article after article on the great evangelist; the modernist *Christian Century* paid

a two-page editorial tribute! Several new biographies, books and booklets appeared.

A high light of this period was the erection of the 12-story Administration Building at 820 North LaSalle Street, long greatly needed to centralize and accommodate expanding business and educational offices scattered in half a dozen buildings over an entire city block. Additional library and classroom space, and radio studios, were likewise sorely needed.

Here again we must bring godly Henry Parsons Crowell to the fore. Dr. Day asked him, "How much did you give toward the Administration Building?" "Well, I suppose about half." (For more than 40 years, he gave to God, 60 to 70 per cent of his income!) During construction, Dr. Houghton urged Mr. Crowell to permit the words "Crowell Hall" to be cut in stone over the arch.

There was silence for perhaps two minutes.

80

Administration Building corner-stone laying, May 27, 1938

Left to right, Dr. Houghton; F. J. Thielbar, architect; Henry P. Crowell, president board of trustees

Crowell Hall unveiling at noon, February 5, 1945, by Miss Mary Crowell (now Mrs. Robert W. Allen), granddaughter of Henry P. Crowell

Women's Building alterations (830 North LaSalle Street), 1939

Then Mr. Crowell lifted his head, and said quietly, "No [pause]; no [pause]; years ago I told the Lord that if He would allow me to make money for His service, I would keep my name out of it, so He could have the glory." [2]

The structure was completed in the fall of 1938, and formally dedicated during Founder's Week of 1939 as the Administration Building. So it remained during Mr. Crowell's lifetime. After his home-going, the building was fittingly renamed Crowell Hall; and thus it has been known to the thousands of students, employees, and visitors who have poured through its doors since then.

[2] *A Christian in Big Business,* the life story of Henry Parsons Crowell, by Dr. R. E. Day; Moody Press, 1954, pp. 177, 205.

Satellite to the erection of Crowell Hall were two other construction (or destruction) jobs. Since the widening of LaSalle Street in 1930 to make way for increasing automobile traffic, remaining Institute buildings were almost out in the street. The solution was simple for the historic Auditorium, formerly Moody Church, on the corner of LaSalle and Chicago. It was razed in 1939, after the completion of the basement of Torrey-Gray Auditorium. For the stately Women's Building, 830 North La-Salle, it wasn't so easy. The front had to be cut off 14 feet, removing or altering the hallway, reception room and Massey Chapel. This was also done in 1939.

Dr. Houghton's administration saw many other changes of various kinds, as M.B.I. grew and developed. The *Student News* (forerunner of today's *Moody Student*) appeared October 18, 1935, "to record human interest stories from various sources of the Moody Bible Institute that otherwise might not be passed on to you." Usually a two-page mimeographed paper at first, it contained interesting and even thrilling stories; *e.g.,* the young couple who drove 3,800 miles one term to attend M.B.I. evening school! They came twice a week from a Wisconsin town 70 miles away.

Then there was the girl who had $14.00, and needed $25.00. This missionary daughter was summoned to the Accounting Department about her overdue bill. She said, "This is all I have, but I have asked my Father to send the remainder."

"So you asked your father to send it; and how soon do you expect it? Within a week?"

"Well, I have asked Him to send it as soon as He can, and I am expecting it very soon," was the confident reply.

Notation was made that the student had written home for the money. The next day she presented a $50.00 check to the cashier. "Oh, your father sent it sooner than you expected, didn't he?"

"Yes, but it was my heavenly Father of whom I asked the money, for I have no earthly father!"

A student worked a while during vacation in a Lancaster, Pa., drugstore, where she had been employed before entering M.B.I. In five hours' work, Harriet Shellehamer talked with 25 people concerning their spiritual condition, four of whom professed to accept Christ as Saviour!

And if you want more thrilling stories like these, revealing the blessing and power of God, go to the M.B.I. Library and browse

August, 1938, class was the first to march through the arch.

B.I.C.A. offices, 843-45 North Wells Street, 1934

through some of the back issues of *Moody Student.*

The December, 1935, class was historic for at least two reasons. Diplomas were awarded by mail, graduation exercises having been omitted because of the scarlet fever epidemic; and Mrs. Addie Whitlock Hale, of Connecticut, a former school teacher and M.B.I. correspondence course student, was graduated at 80, the oldest person ever to receive a diploma here!

Caps and gowns made their first appearance in Institute life when 33 men and women marched to the platform April 23, 1936. Institute colors were used: deep maroon for the caps and gowns themselves, with white trim and tassels. Since then, all-maroon caps and gowns have been adopted, though women also wear white collars.

Two years later, another familiar institution came into being: the school yearbook, the *Arch,* named for the symbolic arch in Crowell Hall through which students enter for training and depart for service.

It was one day about 1938, when Dr. Houghton met young Irwin A. Moon, '26, in Los Angeles. Moon was then a pastor who had originated and developed a remarkable series of demonstrations called "Sermons from Science," in order to present an appealing and challenging Gospel message. Dr. Houghton immediately saw the great potential of this ministry, and suggested a connection with the Institute. As a result of that meeting, a lifetime association was formed between the two that led to Moon's meetings at the San Francisco World's Fair in 1939 and 1940, the great ministry in military installations during World War II, and of course the birth of Moody Institute of Science.

In 1941, the Bible Institute Colportage Association was merged with M.B.I. The Colportage organization had also been founded by D. L. Moody (in 1894) to make available inexpensive Christian books, booklets and tracts. Indeed, literature was provided for free distribution by Christian workers holding services in jails, hospitals and many other institutions in this country, as well as in foreign lands. It had always been a separate organization, though closely associated in motive and message. William Norton, for more than 50 years head of the Colportage work, used to describe it as the "married daughter of the Institute, who had gone to housekeeping over on Wells Street."

In announcing the change, Dr. Houghton said, "We are sure that this union will mean a great increase in every phase of the work done by each of the organizations." Offices were

B.I.C.A. bookstore, 1940

moved from 843 North Wells Street to a part of their present space on the seventh floor of Crowell Hall. The bookstore, however, remained for a time on Wells Street at the corner of Institute Place, part of the present parking lot area.

Student enrollment continued to grow. Evening school reached an all-time high of 1,260 in the fall term of 1940. (Day school maximum to date is 1,057, fall of 1955.) From various backgrounds they came: educational, cultural, national, denominational. Practically every state in the union and many foreign countries were represented almost every year. But all came with one purpose: to know the Word and will of God.

Some came from unsympathetic homes, where they received little or no encouragement. Indeed, some faced bitter opposition. One

"Old Princeton has Nassau, whose steps are held sacred,
And Harvard a yard, and Yale College a fence;
No campus has Moody, but courts and queer alleys,
But leave us that railing, and take the rest hence!"
—*From "The Old Iron Railing," by Dr. Gray*

This famous railing in front of the 153 building has been the scene of many a theological debate—and discussion on other matters too.

After Miss Gretchen Stanberry received her Christian education diploma on August 5, 1941, Dr. Houghton pinned a maroon and white ribbon on Queenie, amid the applause of the audience. This photograph, syndicated by Associated Press, appeared in newspapers from coast to coast.

Other blind persons have attended M.B.I., but Miss Stanberry is apparently the only one ever accompanied by a seeing eye dog. Mrs. Blanche Breckenridge, superintendent of women, got special permission for Queenie to live in the 830 building. One day Queenie came in from a stroll without her mistress. Instead of taking the stairs, she insisted on waiting for the elevator!
Chicago Daily News *photo*

young man was taken to a police station after Sunday school one day because of his desire to attend M.B.I., and the officer on duty was asked "if he could not be put in reform school!" After hearing the complaint, he said to the zealous mother, "Lady, if I had a son like this boy I would be more than proud of him." Then to the young man, "Boy, as long as you follow the Book you have under your arm, you will never go wrong."

One malady that afflicts some students when they first come to M.B.I. is homesickness, and another, for those from the country or small town, is getting used to the big city. One young man from the really wide open spaces of Wyoming had real trouble along these lines. Mr. A. F. Broman, superintendent of men, urged him· to stay awhile and try to get adjusted. Said the student: "You expect me to feel at home here with buildings only a few

feet apart, yet out where I come from, when they begin to build a fence a mile away we feel hemmed in!" In spite of crowded conditions he stayed for two years, until he went into the Navy during World War II.

Here are two thrilling incidents, demonstrating the leading of the Holy Spirit and the power of the Gospel unto salvation, gleaned from one of Mr. James F. Harrison's annual reports. The first reminds one in some ways of an experience in the life of D. L. Moody.

A student could not sleep one night because of his failure to speak to someone about Christ that day. The snowy winter night made him pull the blankets up around him, but there was no peace, so he got up, dressed, prayed for guidance, and went out.

Finding two men in a Chicago Avenue doorway, he gave them tracts and witnessed, but they would not listen. A few blocks far-

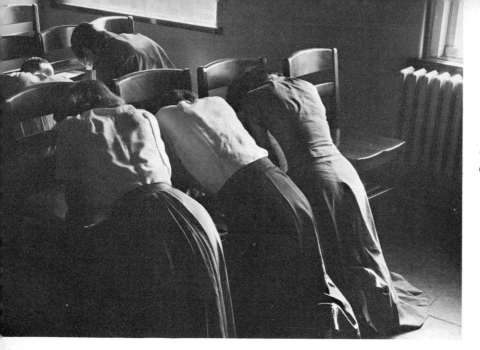

Victories for Christ in Practical Christian Work assignments are won in prayer.

ther, he caught up with a Negro and began by speaking about the swirling white snowflakes and the promise of Isaiah 1:18. After further conversation in the shelter of a nearby building, the man accepted Christ as his Saviour, and the student returned to his room rejoicing; rest and peace were his.

One Saturday morning in chapel, as "Lead Me to Some Soul Today" was sung, a student was asking, "Will God lead me to any soul today?" Late that afternoon she found herself on Clark Street behind a girl wearing rose-colored slacks, a blue shirt and bluish-gray military jacket, blue shoes with red heels, and a blue-figured scarf around her bleached hair. The student felt led to hand her a tract and was soon engaged in serious spiritual conversation, which was continued over supper in a drugstore booth.

The oddly dressed one "had no faith whatsoever—had never been brought up with any." She was in show business, and during the last

An unusual opportunity was afforded M.B.I. for witness and ministry when students were invited to sing Christmas carols in the lobby of City Hall, about 1936. Group included Alvin Hirsch and George Santa.

Men seated and others in photo were city employees.

88

Child evangelism class in Open Door Gospel Center, spring, 1946

three years had been from San Diego to New York dancing. That day she had left her cabaret job, though she had no money, and now wanted to sell some of her dresses to get money for transportation home because of her mother's serious illness.

After lengthy conversation, the show girl felt her need of the Saviour but wanted more time to think it over. They walked together to the 830 building, where the student introduced her new acquaintance to several other students who also witnessed to her. Finally, they formed a prayer circle in one corner of the 830 reception room, first one praying and then another. Then the cabaret dancer, trembling, burst out, "Lord Jesus, come into my heart!" As they rejoiced together in her new-found salvation, she said, "Girls, I'm so happy. Gee whiz, I'm happy! This is the most wonderful night of my life. A miracle has happened—I know I'm a new person!"

The students gave her words of assurance, a

Cook County Hospital group enjoying refreshments in Sweet Shop after last meeting of term, April 10, 1946

Mr. Broman spikes one over the net. This group, including (left to right) George S. Schuler, William Lessel, Dr. Culbertson, and Harry Dixon Loes, was number one team for several years in faculty and staff competition. Occasionally they played students, nearly always beating them. Coach Edward H. Ockert is in center background.

Dr. Fitzwater returns a high one. Tennis court stood on present site of Houghton Hall.

New Testament, a Frances Ridley Havergal book, and more—bus fare home, which at first the new-born child of God refused to take, until told it was tithe money and not actually their own. Later a former student working in Detroit called on her and found her "living a beautiful Christian testimony by word of mouth and life." [3]

Although M.B.I. has not participated in a regular sports league, there have been games, usually basketball or touch football, with other schools on occasion, including Garrett Biblical Institute in Evanston, Wheaton College, North Park College, Chicago Theological Seminary and other schools in the area. For many years, faculty and staff members have played volley ball in the gym at noon, except on Tuesdays when an employee prayer meeting is held. In summer it was a familiar sight to see faculty and staff members as well as students playing tennis on the corner of Chicago Avenue and LaSalle Street. Dr. P. B. Fitzwater, a volley ball enthusiast for many years, was named the outstanding player on the Lawson YMCA team when he was past 70! Finally at 79, he had to substitute walking and other forms of exercise for that game.

[3] Condensed from Practical Christian Work office annual report, September 1, 1938.

90

The coming of World War II brought many changes, notably a rapidly dwindling number of men students. Some buildings were changed to house women, or married couples. It became the custom to sing a patriotic number during Monday morning chapel.[4] The huge service flag flying on LaSalle Street testified to all that hundreds of students and employees were serving in the Armed Forces.

At the outset of the war, M.B.I. launched a drive to reach servicemen for Christ through Irwin A. Moon's Sermons from Science demonstrations and film; Colportage books and tracts, millions of which were distributed by chaplains and others; and *Moody Monthly* magazine, which went to many service reading rooms in America and overseas. The W. W. Shannon and Michael Guido Extension Department team held evangelistic meetings in military and naval installations, distributing

[4] Chapel was changed from Saturday to Monday in 1939 when Institute offices began working a five-day week.

W. W. Shannon (left) and Michael Guido
at Camp McCoy, Wis., 1943

New Testaments to the men and earning the commendation of Navy Secretary Frank Knox.

One of the four heroic chaplains who perished on a sinking troop transport was a former M.B.I. student. Lt. George L. Fox, '23, was aboard the S. S. "Dorchester" when it was tor-

Chapel service in basement of Torrey-Gray Auditorium. This building, seating 1,800, was dedicated during Founder's Week, 1939.

t. George L. Fox, '23, one of the ur chaplains who went down on the S. S. "Dorchester"
U. S. Army photo

Maynard William Tollberg, water tender 2nd class, U.S.N.R., killed in action, January 30, 1943

Lt. Gen. Sir William G. S. Dobbie, G.C.M.G., K.C.B., D.S.O., LL.D.

S. S. "Dwight L. Moody," launched in June, 1943, transported military and commercial cargo in European, African and Pacific war theaters. It is now in the national defense reserve fleet at Beaumont, Tex.

D. L. Moody himself could not conscientiously bear arms, and therefore did not serve in the military during the Civil War.

pedoed and sunk off Greenland in February, 1943. The War Department said, "Fear of the icy water had made many aboard almost helpless. The chaplains calmed their fears and are given credit for saving many men by persuading them to go overboard where there was a chance of rescue." They encouraged the men, prayed with them, helped them into lifeboats and life belts, and at last, in the supreme sacrifice, gave up their own life jackets.

The ship was sinking by the bow when men in the water and in lifeboats saw the chaplains link arms and heard them raise their voices in prayer. They were still praying together on the deck when the ship made its final plunge.

Each chaplain was awarded posthumously the Distinguished Service Cross, and all four were honored by a commemorative three-cent postage stamp issued in 1948.

A native of Lewistown, Pa., Lt. Fox had been pastor of a number of churches in New England. After the war, his widow (formerly Isadore Hurlbut, '23) continued to pastor churches in Vermont.

Another thrilling story from World War II is that of Bill Tollberg. He and his wife, who had both attended evening school during the 1930's, worked together in jails, hospitals and a Chicago mission. When the war broke out, Bill's educational qualifications did not permit him to become a chaplain, so he enlisted in the Navy. Aboard ship, he bore a faithful and fruitful witness.

Then one day it happened, off Guadalcanal. A Japanese torpedo hit Bill's ship, and a shattering explosion released high pressure steam, killing everybody in the engine room but Bill. Severely scalded, partly blinded, he groped his way over the bodies of dead comrades, and with his fast-ebbing strength, closed an oil valve, saving the lives of a number of trapped shipmates. For extraordinary heroism, the Navy Cross was awarded posthumously. But even more precious was this letter from a shipmate: "Even since his death there have been some who have accepted Christ because of his testimony." "He being dead yet speaketh!" And in due time, the Navy further honored him by launching the U. S. S. "Tollberg."

In 1945 Dr. Houghton arranged for Lt. Gen. Sir William G. S. Dobbie and Lady Dobbie to tour the United States under M.B.I. auspices. The distinguished and heroic defender of the island of Malta, so strategically important to Allied power in the Mediterranean, was widely known not only as a great military man but also as a devoted servant of the Lord Jesus Christ.

Their ministry was aimed at middle and upper classes—people from political, business, professional, and social life, largely unreached by the Gospel message. In Washington, D. C., the Dobbies addressed House and Senate breakfast groups and were luncheon guests of Mrs. Franklin D. Roosevelt in the White House, the President then being out of the city. She was so impressed she referred to them three different times in her nationally syndicated newspaper column.

During their four-month tour, they addressed at least 150,000 people in some 40 cities from coast to coast, the largest crowd being 9,000 in Minneapolis. At exclusive clubs, university gatherings, high society teas,

Informal group in 830 reception room. Left to right, seated: Clinton Kinney, Florence Longacre, Virginia Keesey, Cal Didier, and Frances McConkie; standing: George Sweeting and Don Rose. All were Aug. '45 graduates, except Frances, Dec. '46, and Cal, special.

as well as mass meetings, they bore a unique testimony for the Lord Jesus Christ.[5]

The 1945 *Arch* listed almost 500 former students and employees who served in the war, including 15 who made the supreme sacrifice. And, the war over, back to M.B.I. came hundreds of ex-servicemen to pick up where they had left off with their educational program and plans for future Christian work. With them came others just starting their schooling. The proportion of men students rose to its normal of approximately half, and buildings were converted again to men's dormitories to accommodate them. While many men had gone through the horrors of war and even imprisonment in Europe and the Pacific, most made satisfactory adjustment to civilian life at M.B.I. without great difficulty.

But the entire postwar period brought its changes and difficulties. The area around M.B.I. seemed to deteriorate faster than before. Three women's dormitories were located a block and a half away (the 900 building, Wakeman Hall, and the 148 building), and to

[5] Condensed from *Dobbie, Defender of Malta*, by Dr. S. Maxwell Coder, Moody Press, 1946.

Junior class president extends traditional welcome at junior-senior banquet, November 18, 1946, in Moody Memorial Church.

Oh, for the life of a Rec Club officer!

Dr. Houghton once said that at M.B.I., "Pranks and prayers are in proper proportion." Senior prexy (right) hiding out from wild juniors before retreat, which included antics like these.

reach them, girls had to pass the ruins of the Grace M. E. Church at LaSalle and Locust, which had become a rendezvous for tramps. The Institute provided special police protection on LaSalle Street for the safety of students and employees, which is still being done today. The inflation which began then brought the first substantial increase since depression days: a single room with board went up to $10.75 weekly.

But the greatest difficulty for M.B.I. was the illness and death of its president. In the providence of God, Dr. Gray had kept office hours until a week before his death. In fact, on a Friday he spoke to students with unusual power on the work of the Holy Spirit. Two days later, a heart attack; six days afterward, he was with the Lord. But it was destined to be far different for Dr. Houghton.

Dr. Wilbur M. Smith, then a member of the M.B.I. faculty and close associate, gives this intimate and moving account in his biography of Dr. Houghton:

> For 30 years, this strong man had suffered from migraine headaches, which by the early 1940's had become more frequent and painful. In 1945, those who were close to him could at times notice a haggard look in his face, which was sometimes dark, purplish; again, during great pain, pale, almost white.
>
> I remember meeting Dr. Houghton in the arch of the Administration Building one morning about 7 (an early riser, he was often first of all the staff of more than 300 to enter the building). Knowing something of his present sufferings, I quietly asked, "And how are you this morning?" His only answer was, while he seemed to be leaning rather heavily against the brick wall, "I guess I am all right. I did not sleep all night—but, there is work to do."
>
> On June 4, 1946, he suffered a serious heart attack, and was immediately taken to Presbyterian Hospital in Chicago, returning home July 18. Less and less frequently was he able to work in the office. Sometimes he would dress, come downstairs, sit in the lobby (at 399 Fullerton Parkway) for a few

minutes looking out at the street, then go back to his apartment. Large decisions were demanding attention, and he increasingly felt he did not have the strength to wrestle with them.

On August 14, he and Mrs. Houghton flew to Seattle, then went on to Victoria, B. C., for rest and absolute separation from all correspondence and problems. He returned to Chicago in October, but found that the rest had not brought the expected results. Sometimes he would spend a day in the office, sometimes half a day, again only an hour. His last appearance in chapel was November 4, 1946.

Now realizing that he *must* get better, Dr. Houghton went to Hot Springs, Ark., on November 23, by train, Mrs. Houghton following by car. Later they spent about three months in Tucson, Ariz. These were days of great suffering, marked by hemorrhages, utter exhaustion, headaches of increasing intensity, all so discouraging, even for the noblest man.

From April 9-24, 1947, the Houghtons were at Del Mar, Calif., then went to Los Angeles. His absence from the Institute was creating problems which needed his personal attention, and toward the end, since he seemed to be growing better, he made full plans, including train reservations, to return to Chicago and pick up again the great tasks awaiting him. On June 13, he seemed to be exceedingly hopeful, filled with enthusiasm, and more like himself than he had been for months. But that day an unusually severe headache suddenly seized him, the pain of which became almost unbearable. Ice packs were laid one upon another on his throbbing head, without results. That night his heart gave way, unable longer to stand the strain, and early on June 14, 1947, his spirit departed from a body wracked with pain, and he entered into the presence of the Lord whom he had loved and served so faithfully.

The funeral on June 20 was without doubt one of the most remarkable services held for one of God's great servants in our generation. The body lay in state that morning at Moody Bible Institute, where thousands passed before the open bier. In the afternoon, the service at Moody Memorial Church was attended by more than 4,000 persons. Dr. Culbertson said in part:

The message that our Lord had called unto Himself His servant, Dr. Houghton not only left us saddened, it left us stunned. It seemed difficult to pierce the darkness of bewilderment. It was hard to see God's providential care; for the moment it seemed that we were desolate. Then our Heavenly Father began to speak in and through the grief which He permitted to come. We do not need to *see,* it is enough to know; it is better to know, for that knowledge rests in who God is. Sight is limited; knowledge transcends sight. Even when we do not see, ". . . we know that all things work together for good to them that love God, to them who are the called according to his purpose."

And, further, the God of all comfort reminded us of some of the lessons Dr. Houghton was used of Him to impress upon our minds and hearts. For it is as Dr. Irwin Moon observed, Dr. Houghton never entered a room or a life without leaving it full. The shattering sense of loss was only because of our great personal grief; calmer moments prove that we have not lost the warm and strong counsel of this man of God; he, under God, has made a deposit that shall endure.

Dr. Houghton left us a written heritage as well as living memories. To the child of God comes this word:

So this is life, this world with all its pleasures,
   Struggles and tears, a smile, a frown, a sigh,
Friendship so true, and love of kin and neighbor,
   Sometimes 'tis hard to live—always, to die!
The world moves on, so rapidly the living
   The forms of those who disappear replace,
And each one dreams that he will be enduring—
   How soon that one becomes the missing face!

In life or death—and life is surely flying,
   The crib and coffin carved from the self-same tree.
In life or death—and death so soon is coming—
   Escape I cannot, there's no place to flee—
But Thou, O God, hast life that is eternal;
   That life is mine, a gift through Thy dear Son,
Help me to feel its flush and pulse supernal,
   Assurance of the morn when life is done.

Help me to know the value of these hours,
   Help me the folly of all waste to see;
Help me to trust the Christ who bore my sorrows,
   And thus to yield for life or death to Thee.
In all my ways be glorified, Lord Jesus,
   In all my ways guide me with Thine own eye;
Just when and as Thou wilt, use me, Lord Jesus,
   And then for me 'tis Christ, to live or die.[6]

[6] "By Life or By Death" (words only), copyright, 1938, by George S. Schuler; assigned to the Rodeheaver Company, 1959; words used by permission.

Big moment in the life of a music major—senior recital. Lois Jean Allen, Apr. '47, seated at organ in Torrey-Gray Auditorium (now Towner Hall).

Hear a sobbing and pleading heart:

Lead me to some soul today,
　O teach me, Lord, just what to say;
Friends of mine are lost in sin,
　And cannot find their way.
Few there are who seem to care,
　And few there are who pray;
Melt my heart and fill my life,
　Give me one soul today.[7]

Lessons from the life of Dr. Will H. Houghton? Many, many of them! Will you

listen, will you heed the ones mentioned today? There is salvation in the blood of Christ. There is consecration, if we would meet the divine approval upon our earthly journey. There is witnessing with a heart of love. There is confidence in the darkest hour, for God is on the throne. We, therefore, take heart. The God of Moody, of Torrey, of Gray, of Crowell, and of Houghton, still lives!

Burial was at New Bethlehem, Pa., where he had held one of his first pastorates.[8]

[7] "Lead Me to Some Soul Today," words by Dr. Houghton, music by Wendell P. Loveless, in memory of D. L. Moody. Copyright, 1936, by Mr. Loveless; used by permission.

[8] Condensed from Chapter XXII of *Will H. Houghton A Watchman on the Wall*, by Dr. Wilbur M. Smith. Copyright, 1951, by William B. Eerdmans Publishing Company; used by permission.

Ruth Weinmann, Apr. '47, gets introduced to Lake Michigan (almost) by Dorothy Wade, Dec. '47, and Lillian Chipley, Apr. '47.

1947 *Arch* staff at one of those interminable meetings required to put the yearbook together

Apt to teach

I. Tim. 3:2

WILLIAM CULBERTSON

1942-

On September 1, 1942, after successful pastorates, Dr. William Culbertson became dean of education at M.B.I. He had been elected bishop of the New York and Philadelphia synod of the Reformed Episcopal Church when only 31 years old. For some years he was a member of the board of trustees and a lecturer at Reformed Episcopal Seminary, Philadelphia, and also instructor at Philadelphia School of the Bible.

During Dr. Houghton's illness, increasing responsibilities fell upon Dr. Culbertson. In 1947, for the first time, he had to preside at Founder's Week. Upon Dr. Houghton's homegoing, the trustees in emergency meeting June 19, 1947, named Dr. Culbertson acting president.

A few months later, there could be no doubt as to the leading of the Lord. On February 4, 1948, the trustees elected Dr. Culbertson president of M.B.I. The announcement, made that day at a special meeting of all employees, was greeted with hearty applause and the spontaneous singing of the doxology.

Dr. Culbertson said, "I cannot take Dr. Houghton's place. But I want to be in God's will and in the place God wants me to be. Moody Bible Institute can be a power for God as each one of us is in the place God can use us. I know we will experience the power of God as we go on with Him. The God of Moody, of Torrey, of Gray, of Crowell, and of Houghton, still lives!" On May 13, Dr.

Culbertson was formally inaugurated to the high office he has held with such distinction ever since—and with the unanimous love and esteem of faculty, staff, students, and alumni through the years.

M.B.I. participated in a historic event when representatives of 40 Bible schools meeting at Winona Lake, Ind., in October, 1947, formed the Accrediting Association of Bible Institutes and Bible Colleges (now the Accrediting Association of Bible Colleges). The purpose was to standardize Bible school credits and courses; raise educational standards in general; and be of mutual help and endeavor to maintain the distinctive contribution of the Bible institute as a solid and powerful spiritual force. Today the organization lists 28 accredited schools, including M.B.I., and 12 associate institutions.

The postwar period, which brought such a great influx of veterans to M.B.I. as well as other schools, saw a number of changing educational patterns. There was an increasing emphasis upon education everywhere. More and more people coming to M.B.I. had some college or other higher education. (Of the 405 new students entering in the fall of 1958, one-fourth had some training beyond secondary school, including 35 college graduates and 47 others with from one to four years of college.) M.B.I. had to be sure its academic standards were sufficiently high to meet the increasing demands of the modern world, meanwhile

Dr. Culbertson, 1942

LaSalle Street buildings looked like this at beginning of Dr. Culbertson's administration.

Faculty and special instructors, March, 1943

Left to right, seated: William H. Lee Spratt, Dr. P. B. Fitzwater, Miss Angelyn G. Dantuma, A. F. Broman, Dr. Will H. Houghton, Dr. William Culbertson, Miss Ruby Ann Jackson, Dr. Max I. Reich, Dr. William H. Hockman.

Second row: Dr. Robert Heurlin, Dr. Elgin S. Moyer, George E. Leslie, Nathan J. Stone, Dr. John H. Cable, Dr. John R. Riebe, Dr. Kenneth S. Wuest, Dr. Warren Filkin, Dr. Thomas Cottrell, Carl J. Schumacher, Dr. Harold L. Lundquist.

Third row: James F. Harrison, Miss Helen Needham, Miss Lois LeBar, Miss Eleanor Gemberling, Miss Margaret Gordon, Miss H. Adella Dunlap, Miss Ella Wubbena, Mrs. Frances C. Allison, Miss Edna E. Fritsch, Miss Gladys Mary Talbot, Mrs. W. H. Hockman, Wendell P. Loveless

Back row: Harold E. Garner, Alfred Holzworth, Frank Earnest, J. Harry Johnson, George S. Schuler, Guy C. Latchaw, Talmage J. Bittikofer, Harry Dixon Loes, John D. Thomas, Edward H. Ockert

Not shown are Miss Grace Darling, Dr. G. Allen Fleece, Dr. Wilbur M. Smith and Dr. William McCarrell

Of those pictured, 12 are still active at M.B.I. today, a number of others having been retired. At least eleven have gone to be with the Lord.

Bible school representatives meeting at Winona Lake
to form accrediting association

maintaining the proper balance between the spiritual and scholastic aspects.

While M.B.I. has, almost from the very beginning, trained pastors, missionaries, evangelists and musicians, the role of the Christian education worker has become increasingly important in recent years. Today many churches have a full-time Christian education director, though sometimes this is part of the function of an assistant pastor or other worker. The Christian education course has therefore become increasingly important in recent years.

The newest course at M.B.I. was born during the postwar years, the result of the vision of Paul Robinson, Aug. '36. After a number of years in the pastorate, he became burdened for the mission field, especially for the use of

modern planes and radios to facilitate the work of isolated missionaries. He then planned to go to South America as a missionary airman, but three days after his first solo flight came Pearl Harbor, and he was grounded for the duration. When at last it appeared that he could not go himself, he set about planning a flight training program for missionaries, which he submitted to his alma mater. Back came an invitation to present it in person to the board of trustees at its next meeting. He appeared with fear and trembling—"just a country preacher with an idea that probably wasn't even practical"—but imagine his surprise when one trustee offered to donate the first two training planes!

In 1946 Mr. Robinson joined the M.B.I.

101

faculty, beginning with three students in a 50-hour aviation course for missionaries and others who would use it in full-time Christian work. Within a few years, the present three-year missionary technical course developed, in which missionary technical specialists are trained, majoring in either aviation or radio and communications. (Aviation majors spend an extra year in post-graduate work.) Today nearly all the 100-odd graduates are either serving on the foreign field, or definitely planning toward that end. Operating under service organizations such as Wycliffe Bible Translators Jungle Aviation and Radio Service, Missionary Aviation Fellowship, and Missionary Engineering (communications), as well as various other mission boards, they provide two of the isolated missionary's greatest needs: transportation and communications, not only in life-and-death emergencies, but in such daily routine matters as getting groceries, other supplies and mail, or advice on various problems in the work.

The missionary technical course thus takes its place with seven other basic M.B.I. courses: general Bible, missionary, pastors, music, Christian education, Christian education-music, and Jewish missions.

The fall of 1951 witnessed one of the greatest changes in the history of M.B.I.: beginning of the semester plan. Originally, the Institute operated twelve months a year; students entered at any time, stayed as long as they could. However, for some 40 years, the term plan had been in effect, with school in session almost eleven months, and with three graduations annually: April, August, and December. New students entered each term; there was increasing difficulty in transferring to and from other schools, as well as in other ways. Further, the

Here Dr. Wuest gives some down-to-earth golden nuggets from the Greek New Testament.

Dr. C. Norman Bartlett, teaching Bible doctrine, Torrey-Gray Auditorium, 1949

Church history class with Dr. Elgin S. Moyer

Aircraft engines require the constant attention of well-trained mechanics. Tech course students receive practical experience in all types of maintenance.

Rebuilding and modifying of aircraft is a vital part of the missionary airman's work. Here students learn how in hangar and shop classes.

Part of MBI fleet of training planes

Working on experiment in theoretical lab

Advanced radio theory class, radio and communications section of tech course

Building a missionary base station transmitter in practical lab

Evening sessions of Founder's Week pack Moody Church. In 1951, Dr. Billy Graham spoke twice one night; about 5,000 attended each time with many turned away.

student load had grown to an average of 12 subjects, with most classes meeting one hour a week.

In 1951, the curriculum was completely re-arranged to eliminate duplication, and provide fewer subjects meeting oftener during the week. The traditional two-year training was discontinued; all courses require three years. Two school semesters run from early in September until about the first week of June; thereafter, two successive three-week summer school sessions are held. The summer also provides time for additional employment, study, field work required in some courses, and many opportunities for service in Bible conferences and other forms of ministry. Faculty members (except those teaching in summer school) likewise have the summer for additional study or other ministry.

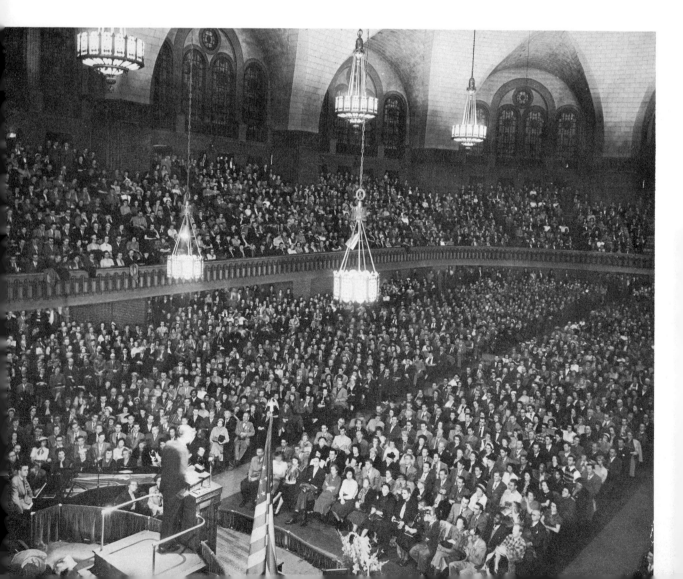

On July 31, 1953, the last term-plan graduation was held, and the transition was complete. This class also goes down in history as probably the only one in which husband, wife, and son (or daughter) have been graduated at the same time. Ray and Vera Rennels, and their son, Bill, received diplomas that night— the men from the pastors course, Mrs. Rennels from the general Bible. They had all worked for M.B.I. during student days too, but neither employment, family nor anything else interfered with studies; father and mother won honors in scholarship, and son high honors!

As we have seen, music has always played an important part in the work of M.B.I. In 1946, James P. Davies of the music faculty organized the Moody Chorale, replacing the old Auditorium Choir. The following year, Don Hustad, formerly of the WMBI staff, became director. To date, almost half a million persons have heard the Chorale in some 700 engagements all over the U. S. A. and many parts of Canada and Europe. In addition, they have ministered to countless others in radio and TV appearances.

The Chorale provides invaluable training for music students in great choral literature, as well as familiar hymn settings. Its ministry has

Bill Pearce interviews Billy Graham during Founder's Week, 1951.

been greatly blessed in the edification of Christians, evangelization of the unsaved and, incidentally, the publicizing of M.B.I., since many young people have been called to the Institute after hearing the Chorale.

In 1954, the group toured the British Isles, giving more than 50 concerts. Urgent requests for a return trip from pastors throughout Britain encouraged the planning of a second tour,

High point of Founder's Week is alumni banquet in the dining room. These students were among the last ones to have heard D. L. Moody personally.

Moody Chorale, 1946

which took the Chorale into six European countries in the summer of 1958, ministering to more than 60,000 people. In London, some 3,000 filled the magnificent Royal Festival Hall; other capacity audiences included Glasgow (3,400), Edinburgh (3,000), Brighton (5,000), and Frankfurt (2,400). Secular and religious press, pastors and others paid high tribute to the musical excellence of the "missionaries in song."

During the school year, the Chorale makes two extended concert tours and many local appearances, particularly Founder's Week and the Commencement Musicale. The 1959 season included a performance in the North Shore Festival with members of the Chicago Symphony Orchestra. Two Chorale LP albums have been released by Word Records.

Another important event of 1951 was the first postwar construction at M.B.I.—the ten-story women's dormitory, Houghton Hall, on the site of the old M.B.I. Auditorium. This resulted in a succession of moves, women vacating 830 and smaller buildings, and men moving from 153 into what was formerly "no man's land," the 830 building. Visitors still remark occasionally about how unusual it seems for women to be using the south end of the dining room, and men the north end, just the opposite of the arrangement for so many years! (At two meals daily, seating is mixed, but at breakfast men and women sit separately.)

Moody Chorale in Easter sunrise service, Hollywood Bowl, Los Angeles, 1953
Moody Institute of Science photo

Some 10,000 heard the Chorale in the Botanical Gardens, Belfast, in 1954.

More than an hour before the concert, this crowd was gathering outside Christ Church, Blackpool, England, 1958.

F. Neil Wilson, Jan. '52, gives out the Word of God in tract form.

House to house visitation: scriptural, practical, profitable.

Houghton Hall cornerstone laying, June 22, 1951

Pictured are Gustave Orth, architect; Mrs. Will H. Houghton; Frank F. Taylor, chairman, M.B.I. board of trustees; and Dr. Culbertson. Cornerstone verse: "He that winneth souls is wise" (Prov. 11:30).

Erection of Torrey-Gray Auditorium and Doane Memorial Building, 1954. Cornerstone of latter was laid commencement day, June 11.

Because of a shortage of dormitory space for men, it was necessary to lease an entire floor of the Lawson YMCA, two blocks away, for M.B.I. students. But contrary to rumor, the historic 153 building is not, and never has been, condemned. It is no longer used as a dormitory because cost of maintenance for the available space makes it impractical. Nearly all of the first three floors are still in use for offices and classrooms.

Even now, an occasional former student coming back to visit likes to make his way up to the deserted fourth or fifth floor, back to a Bethel where he lived during student days and won spiritual victories.

The bookstore opened for business October 30, 1951, in its bright new quarters on the first floor of Houghton Hall. Within two years, M.B.I. had acquired all the remaining property in the block from Chicago to Chestnut, and LaSalle to Wells. Temporarily, the area from Houghton Hall to Wells Street, and north to Institute Place, is being used as a parking lot. One wonders now how we ever did get along when Institute Place was the only parking area for employees, students, and visitors!

Through the years M.B.I. has sought to be as right in its accounting as in its doctrine. It has, for example, always kept faith with its donors by using specified gifts for the pur-

Capacity crowd filled Torrey-Gray Auditorium for dedication service, February 1, 1955.
Record number, about 53,000, attended Founder's Week that year.

Chicago Sun-Times *photo*

poses indicated. The building fund is deposited in a separate bank from the operating fund. Even if there were no money on hand to meet the payroll in any month, the Institute would not borrow from the building fund for this purpose.

Incidentally, seldom at the beginning of a month are sufficient operating funds on hand for payroll and other expenses that month. But the Lord provides, day by day. The Institute does not go into debt for its buildings; money is either on hand or in sight before M.B.I. begins construction.

From 1939 on, gifts specified for buildings

had accumulated toward the completion of Torrey-Gray Auditorium. Then a gift from the family of the famous composer, Dr. William Howard Doane, together with a sizable bequest designated for buildings, made possible the erection of the new music building, and also provided the organ for the main auditorium. Previous plans were revised, and the William Howard Doane Memorial Building, providing new music facilities, was erected adjacent to Torrey-Gray Auditorium, which was also finished. Work began immediately after Founder's Week, 1954, and was completed in time for dedication the following Founder's Week.

In reviewing the past, and looking forward to the future, D.V., of the "school that D. L. Moody founded," Dr. S. Maxwell Coder, vice-president and dean of education, says:

God has been pleased to give to Moody Bible Institute a place of strategic importance in today's world.

Who, for example, could evaluate the influence of the Institute simply as a citadel of evangelical Christianity, standing in the heartland of America, and known the world over because of its testimony to the Bible as the Word of God and its adherence to the faith of our fathers?

Just as its historic stand for the truth has encouraged individual believers for nearly 75 years, so the work of the Institute continues to strengthen the church in all its branches. From the school flows a widening stream of Christian leaders, well taught in the Bible and experienced in its practical application to life.

Half of them are now going to the foreign field, half to the various arms of the church at home.

The Institute brings hope throughout the world for many of the problems facing mankind. There is no force for good to compare with the millions of nationals in every land who trust Christ and seek to honor the Word of God because of the spiritual impact of missionaries trained at this school and at the hundreds of other Bible institutes, many of which under God have been patterned after this one, and which now cover the globe.

This is indeed a tree of God's planting. Like the tree of life in Revelation 22, Moody Bible Institute has branched and blossomed and borne many kinds of fruit. Its leaves are for the healing of the nations. Its various ministries, and the sturdy main trunk which is the school, form one of the last best hopes of mankind offered today by the people of God on the earth.

Class of 1955, first to be graduated in completed Torrey-Gray Auditorium

Life at M. B. I. Today

Mr. Broman leading voluntary Thursday night prayer meeting in Norton Hall lounge

Weekly voluntary prayer meeting in Houghton Hall dormitory room

Mrs. Lillian Robinson giving lesson on William Howard Doane memorial organ, Torrey-Gray Auditorium

Daily assembly over, students hurry from Torrey-Gray Auditorium to next class.

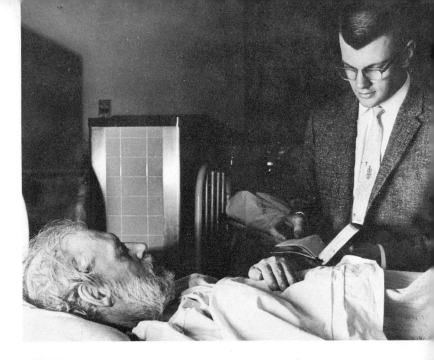

Tom Constable deals with patient in Cook County Hospital, largest institution of its kind in the world.

Skid row habitué hears the old, old story from Douglas McCormack.

Carolyn Morrison bears good news for Cook County Hospital patient.

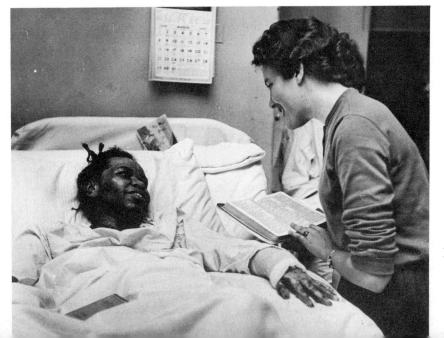

113

The Gospel of Christ is still "the power of God unto salvation," as proclaimed by this group at the West Side Gospel Mission.

MBI group returning from rescue mission assignment.

Things are never dull when a Hi C group meets. MBI students conduct many meetings weekly with young people's groups like this one.

Students conduct D.V.B.S. at North Clark Street mission near MBI.

Gene Brack jumps high to spike one in senior-sophomore sports night match.

Time out from studies for a fast game of doubles in Houghton Hall game room.

Bill Newell tries to avoid Bill Nehrke's tackle as junior-senior team plays sophomores.

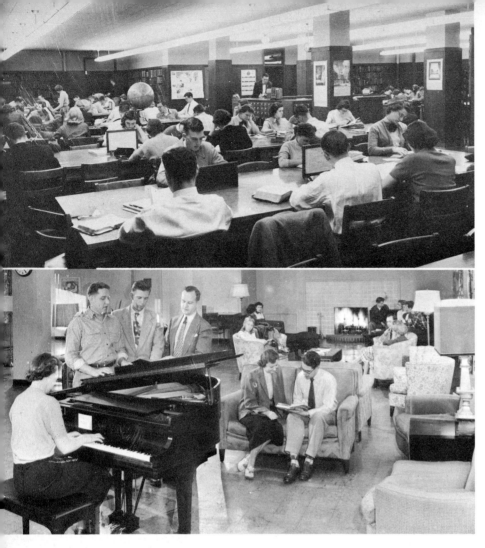

MBI library contains about 53,000 volumes, more than 300 periodicals. Facilities are used by some 2,000 students annually, as well as many faculty and staff members, and visitors.

Informal groups enjoy homelike atmosphere in Houghton Hall lounge.

One of the newest extra-curricular activities is Spanish Club, with Robert Cook as faculty advisor. Most members plan to become missionaries in Spanish-speaking countries.

Class taught by Harold R. Cook, missions instructor, who spent many years as missionary in South America.

Dining room provides part-time employment for many students including Carolyn Riddle.

George Verwer briefs a group of fellow students for service in Mexico during vacation.

Mealtime is always a happy time of fellowship at MBI. A maximum of about 850 persons are served at one meal.

Doctrinal Statement

In view of the present unrest concerning doctrinal questions within the sphere of evangelical Christianity, and to answer inquiries regarding the position of the Moody Bible Institute thereupon, be it *Resolved,* That this Board of Trustees places on record the following statement of faith as that to which its members severally subscribe, and to which it requires the subscription of the members of the faculty of the Educational Branch and all the official heads of the Institute, to wit:

ARTICLE I: God is a Person who has revealed Himself as a Trinity in unity, Father, Son and Holy Spirit—three Persons and yet but one God (Deut. 6:4; Matt. 28:19; I Cor. 8:6).

ARTICLE II: The Bible, including both the Old and the New Testaments, is a divine revelation, the original autographs of which were verbally inspired by the Holy Spirit (II Tim. 3:16; II Pet. 1:21).

ARTICLE III: Jesus Christ is the image of the invisible God, which is to say, He is Himself very God; He took upon Him our nature, being conceived by the Holy Ghost and born of the Virgin Mary; He died upon the cross as a substitutionary sacrifice for the sin of the world; He arose from the dead in the body in which He was crucified; He ascended into heaven in that body glorified, where He is now, our interceding High Priest; He will come again personally and visibly to set up His kingdom and to judge the quick and the dead (Col. 1:15; Phil. 2:5-8; Matt. 1:18-25; I Pet. 2:24, 25; Luke 24; Heb. 4:14-16; Acts 1:9-11; I Thess. 4:16-18; Matt. 25:31-46; Rev. 11:15-17; 20:4-6, 11-15).

ARTICLE IV: Man was created in the image of God but fell into sin, and, in that sense, is lost; this is true of all men, and except a man be born again he cannot see the kingdom of God; salvation is by grace through faith in Christ who His own self bare our sins in His own body on the tree; the retribution of the wicked and unbelieving and the reward of the righteous are everlasting, and as the reward is conscious, so is the retribution (Gen. 1:26, 27; Rom. 3:10, 23; John 3:3; Acts 13:38, 39; 4:12; John 3:16; Matt. 25:46; II Cor. 5:1; II Thess. 1:7-10.)

ARTICLE V: The Church is an elect company of believers baptized by the Holy Spirit into one body; its mission is to witness concerning its Head, Jesus Christ, preaching the gospel among all nations; it will be caught up to meet the Lord in the air ere He appears to set up His kingdom (Acts 2:41; 15:13-17; Eph. 1:3-6; I Cor. 12:12, 13; Matt. 28:19, 20; Acts 1:6-8; I Thess. 4:16-18).

Adopted at the annual meeting of the Board of Trustees, October, 1928.

118

Moody Alumni Association

In a wonderful way, God has been pleased to bless and use former students of M.B.I. To date, nearly 65,000 persons, coming from every state in the Union and many foreign lands, have departed to serve Him around the world. In this country, Moody alumni are enjoying a fruitful ministry as pastors, evangelists, musicians, home missionaries, officials of Bible institutes and colleges, mission boards and conferences. Some of them over the years have been instrumental in founding schools and other organizations which continue to enjoy the blessing of God. Here at M.B.I., more than half the full-time employees are former students.

As nearly as we can tell, 10 per cent of all Protestant foreign missionaries from North America have had some training here. More than 4,000 have gone to foreign fields in 96 countries under 214 mission boards; 17 of them wear the martyr's crown.

A very important factor to any school is the continuing interest of its alumni. Here at the Institute we are particularly blessed in this connection. Many former students go on to college or seminary, but often Moody is the one school toward which they feel the greatest loyalty.

This strong loyalty and devotion is due in no small measure to the work of the Alumni Association, ministering to 33,000 members through its bimonthly *Alumni News,* radio programs on WMBI and other stations, summer conferences at Winona Lake, Ind., and Sandy Cove, Md., and various other alumni meetings and rallies. The Alumni Association also receives more than 600 calls for Christian workers and makes some 300 placements annually.

In less than a decade, the number of organized local fellowships has grown from 5 to 85; alumni giving has increased from $109,000 to more than $218,000 in 1958.

In 1916, A. F. Gaylord, H. W. Pope and Dr. P. B. Fitzwater organized the Alumni Association. The following have served as national presidents:

G. A. Briegleb	1917-19
Ethan E. White	1919-20
John F. Rake	1920-23
C. R. Scafe	1923-26
George M. Landis	1926-31
J. E. Congdon	1931-33
Norman H. Camp	1933-34
A. G. Annette	1934-37
Paul L. Arnold	1937-38
William H. Lee Spratt	1938-44
John S. Ironside	1944-46
Lawrence E. Pearson	1946-49
Al B. Smith	1950-54
William E. Kuhnle	1954-58
Robert A. Cook	1958-

The Thomas S. Smith trophy is awarded annually to an outstanding former student. The following have been so honored:

P. B. Fitzwater	1951
Robert A. Cook	1952
Guy W. Playfair	1953
Theresa Worman	1954
Walter A. Ohman	1955
William R. McCarrell	1956
Clarence W. Jones	1957
A. F. Broman	1958
Lois E. and Mary E. LeBar	1959

Dr. Fitzwater receives first alumnus-of-the-year award from Al Smith, while Mrs. Fitzwater and Mr. Lockyer look on.

Dr. Robert A. Cook
President

Rev. Herbert Lockyer, Jr.
Executive Secretary

Institute Ministries

MOODY PRESS

Founded in 1894 by D. L. Moody, the Bible Institute Colportage Association began largely with the Moody Colportage Library books, 128-page paper bound editions of sermons by Moody, Spurgeon and others. These evangelistic, doctrinal, and devotional messages met a ready and wide acceptance, proving the wisdom of Moody's idea to make good Christian literature available inexpensively.

The paper missionaries were provided free to Christian workers in jails, hospitals, and many other institutions, as well as to foreign missionaries. They were also sold door-to-door by hundred of colporteurs over the country.

As time went on, other books, booklets and tracts were added to the list. In 1941, the organization was merged with M.B.I. as Moody Press. Today it publishes more than 1,000 titles, operates three bookstores, as well as a large retail mail business, and sells through bookstores all over the country.

Moody Press has pioneered in a number of ventures, including reprinting the Wycliffe series of Christian classics, and helping to found the Christian Booksellers Association.

MOODY LITERATURE MISSION

Moody Literature Mission, originally operated as the B.I.C.A. Book Funds, supplies free or at subsidized cost 10,000,000 pieces of literature a year, printed in some 60 languages and reaching nationals of 140 countries.

An important innovation in recent years is the revolving fund, under which a grant of money is made to a mission or other group in a foreign country for printing a particular job. The material is then sold, perhaps at subsidized cost, and the receipts go back into the same fund for other printing, to be used over and over again. It is much more efficient in every way to translate and print in foreign lands, than to do it in this country and ship abroad.

Another innovation is Gospel ads in newspapers, reaching even behind the iron curtain, and bringing hundreds of responses in different countries.

RADIO

The first WMBI license, granted July 28, 1926, permitted operation of a 500-watt station a few hours a day. Today WMBI operates (1110 kc) a 5,000-watt secondary station on a clear channel from daylight to dark every day in the year. Its license is commercial, but the station is operated on a non-commercial educational basis; not a minute of time has ever been sold in more than 100,000 hours on the air.

In the Chicago area, there are 24 AM broadcasting stations, including five of 50,000 watts. Some are on the air much longer than WMBI, a few of them operating 24 hours a day. Yet WMBI has, on occasion, been listed among the top ten stations in this area. (Sur-

Moody Bookstore, LaSalle St. and Chicago Ave., provides wide selection of Christian literature and supplies, handling an estimated 160,000 customer transactions yearly.

Street preaching in India, prior to sale of Bibles and Gospels, the latter furnished by M. L. M. Note idols in background.

Moody Literature Mission funds provided this "pedicab" library mounted on bicycle, in Formosa.

In 10 years, Moody Literature Mission has placed about 120,-000 library sets of Christian books in public schools, mostly in rural areas. Many of these communities have no Sunday school or church.

Student ensemble broadcasting from WMBI studio.
Photo by John Ingram

veys are, of course, made by several different organizations, and ratings may change from month to month.)

More than 100 employees (mostly part-time) provide classical music, news, sermons, sacred music, women's and children's features, and dramatic and variety programs for an estimated 200,000 listeners. During letter week each January, some 20,000 of them write to express their appreciation, and receive an attractive souvenir calendar in return. But throughout the year, letters are received telling of salvation and other blessings as a result of WMBI programs.

The radio ministry is expanding under the blessing of God. At present, programs produced in WMBI studios are heard by tape recording on about 50 other stations in this country and foreign lands. In 1958, Christian businessmen of Cleveland, Ohio, bought and turned over to M.B.I. for operation WCRF-FM, a 21,500-watt station now broadcasting 60 hours weekly on 103.3 mc to a growing audience. Another station, WDLM (1,000-watts FM), under construction at Moline, Ill., is scheduled to go on the air early in 1960.

MOODY INSTITUTE
OF SCIENCE

Dr. Irwin A. Moon, '26, began his famous Sermons from Science, proclaiming the Gospel through electronic demonstrations, under M.B.I. auspices in 1938. One of the most thrilling demonstrations has been the taking of a million volts of electricity through his body. Early in World War II he produced his first film, *They Live Forever,* utilizing war-time scenes and incidents, including the experience of Eddie Rickenbacker's men on the raft in the

123

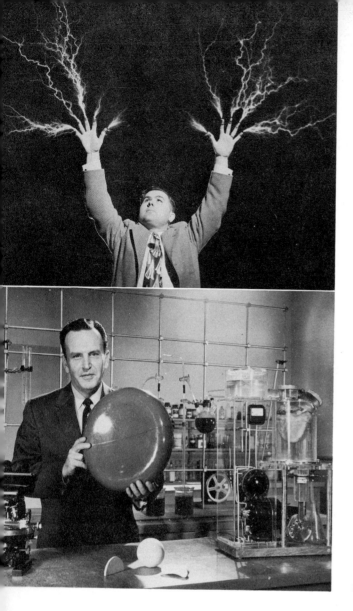

and other institutions. For example, the general superintendent of U. S. Steel's Gary works, largest in the world, used many of them at staff meetings.

Nearly 60,000 letters were received from viewers of two series of M.I.S. films shown on many TV stations throughout the country. It was estimated that millions were reached with the Gospel through these unique programs, adapted from Gospel science and children's adventure films.

Educational films are meeting a wide acceptance at all levels from elementary to college age. Subjects covered range from astronomy and biology to electronics and social science.

MOODY MONTHLY

The *Institute Tie* began publication bi-weekly in 1891 as a combination student-employee-alumni-general circulation paper, but was discontinued the following year. In September, 1900, it appeared again (with different format but the same name), and has been published continuously and monthly ever since.

A. P. Fitt, D. L. Moody's son-in-law, was the first editor of the new series; A. F. Gaylord was treasurer, and William Norton business manager. In 1910 it became the *Christian Workers Magazine,* and in 1920 the *Moody Bible Institute Monthly.* The present name was adopted in 1938.

Pacific. This film, many copies of which were given to chaplains, had a great ministry among servicemen.

The first Gospel science film for general release, *God of Creation,* was produced in 1946 by the newly founded Moody Institute of Science, at 11428 Santa Monica Boulevard, West Los Angeles 25, California. Since then, more than 115 other films and filmstrips have followed, including Gospel science, teacher training, missionary, Bible prophecy, and Bible adventure and science adventure for children.

These have been widely used in business and industry, Armed Forces, churches, schools,

Modern high speed rotary presses produce *Moody Monthly*, the Christian service magazine. *Photo by Kable Printing Co., Mt. Morris, Ill.*

This Christian service family magazine now has an all-time high circulation of more than 100,000. Its many features include news reports, devotional, Bible study, evangelistic, and how-to-do-it articles. Its popular style ranges from "In the Study," by Dr. Wilbur M. Smith, a regular department for pastors and other serious students, to the Youth Supplement, and Moody Monthly Junior for children.

EXTENSION DEPARTMENT

In 1897, the Extension Department was instituted to stimulate Bible study, evangelism and Christian service. For many years, its activities included a weekly Union Bible Class in Chicago, attended by 1,000 or more, as well as noonday services in downtown theaters and tent meetings to reach the masses.

Over the years such well-known men as Dr. H. A. Ironside, Dr. Carl Armerding, and others have served on the Extension staff, which enjoyed a rich ministry of evangelism and Bible teaching in churches and summer conferences all over the country.

Today the Extension Department has five full-time field men holding evangelistic meetings and Bible conferences in response to invitations from churches of many denominations. In 1958, they held a total of 987 meetings, ministering to 117,000.

Extension Department makes many of the arrangements for Founder's Week and other Institute conferences. It also schedules hundreds of faculty, staff, and student team engagements both in Chicago and elsewhere. For 1958, these meetings drew a total attendance of nearly 200,000.

Rev. Philip R. Newell in Bible teaching ministry at Lockwood Bible Church, Chicago.

Rev. David Dyke, pastor of Roseland Evangelical Mission Church, Chicago, teaches Correspondence School class in *Keys to Better Living for Parents*.

CORRESPONDENCE SCHOOL

In 1901 a Correspondence School was added for the convenience of those who could not attend either day or evening school. At present, 33 courses are available in Bible study (from elementary to advanced), Christian living, and Christian service.

The basic Bible series includes such courses as *Good News, First Steps in the Christian Faith,* and *God's Will for Your Life*. Intermediate and advanced courses provide instruction in certain books of the Bible, as well as Bible survey, doctrine, and analysis, including the comprehensive *Scofield Bible Correspondence Course*. Other areas of special interest include church history, prophecy, personal work, practical English, and teacher training. For certain advanced courses, credit is given in day or evening school.

In his small upstairs room in England, an invalid for seventeen years completed some of the longest and most difficult courses. Paralyzed in body, having the use of one arm and one forearm, and forced to be in darkness for weeks because of his eyes, he was able to say, "My Bible is to me a new and living Book, that I owe, by the grace of God, to the correspondence studies of the Moody Bible Institute." A young man in Tennessee wrote, "Through all my years of college and seminary, I owe my spiritual life and my present fundamentalist beliefs to your courses. I thank God for them." Thousands of other testimonies from all over the world have been given to the value of this systematic Bible study at home.

Groups in churches and many other institutions have been organized under the class study plan. Students receive personal attention through individually graded examinations and constructive criticism and suggestions.

Correspondence work is also offered in co-operation with WMBI, Chicago, and WCRF-FM, Cleveland, in the Radio School of the Bible.

Index